PLEASURE, POWER,
AND
TECHNOLOGY

PERSPECTIVES ON GENDER

Editorial Board:

Kay Deaux, CUNY Graduate School and University Center
Myra Marx Ferree, University of Connecticut
Virginia Sapiro, University of Wisconsin—Madison

Volume 1: *Pleasure, Power, and Technology: Some Tales of Gender, Engineering, and the Cooperative Workplace,*

Sally Hacker

Forthcoming:

Captives of Influence: Women's Place in Modern Japan, Charlotte O'Kelly and Larry Carney

Black Feminist Thought, Patricia Hill Collins

Gender Consciousness and Politics, Sue Tolleson Rinehart

Postindustrial Feminism, Angela Miles

Convicted Rapists, Diana Scully

Women, Sexuality, and Feminist Theory, Christine Overall

Black and White Women in the Professions, Natalie Sokoloff

PLEASURE, POWER, AND TECHNOLOGY

Some Tales of Gender, Engineering, and the Cooperative Workplace

Sally Hacker

Boston
UNWIN HYMAN
London Sydney Wellington

Unwin Hyman, Inc.
8 Winchester Place, Winchester, MA 01890, USA

Published by the Academic Division of
Unwin Hyman, Ltd.
15/17 Broadwick Street, London W1V 1FP, UK

Allen & Unwin Australia Pty Ltd,
8 Napier Street, North Sydney, NSW 2060, Australia

Allen & Unwin (New Zealand) Ltd, in association with the Port Nicholson
Press Ltd, Compusales Building, 75 Ghuznee Street,
Wellington 1, New Zealand

First published in 1989

Library of Congress Cataloging-in-Publication Data

Hacker, Sally, 1936–1988
    Pleasure, power, and technology : some tales of gender,
engineering, and the cooperative workplace / Sally Hacker.
    p. cm. –– (Perspectives on gender; v. 1)
    Bibliography: p.
    Includes index.
    ISBN 0-04-445096-6. ISBN 0-04-445204-7 (pbk.)
    1. Women—Employment—Effect of technological innovations on.
    2. Women in cooperative societies—United States. 3. Women in
cooperative societies—Great Britain. 4. Cooperative
societies—Spain—Mondragon. I. Title. II. Series
    HD6053, H17 1989
    334'.89042—dc 19   88–25985 CIP

British Library Cataloguing in Publication Data

Hacker, Sally
    Pleasure, power and technology: some tales
    of gender, engineering, and the cooperative
    workplace.—(Perspectives on gender; v. 1).
    1. Industrial cooperatives. Role of women
    I. Title   II. Series
    334.6

    ISBN 0-04-445096-6   0-04-445204-7 pbk

Typeset in 11 on 12 point Goudy by Columns Reading and printed in Great
Britain by Billing and Sons, London and Worcester

CONTENTS

ACKNOWLEDGMENT

Many people helped Sally write this book. Many more influenced the life from which the book springs. Acknowledging everyone who counted would have been a large task, but it was one Sally anticipated with pleasure. She hoped to credit all those to whom she felt debts of love, affection, and gratitude, beginning with the families that nurtured and sustained her. Sadly, her final illness left her unequal to the task. In lieu of anything more formal, then, let this simple statement suffice: Heartfelt thanks to everyone who helped Sally become the person she was and write the book she did.

FOREWORD

The fantastic human ability to transform nature has in the last 150 years produced material marvels and great wealth and, at the same time, helped to push world society into a perilous situation, in which starvation, killing, and torture are commonplace and the realistic potential exists for obliterating all human life. Is this where the promise of liberal capitalism has led us? How are we to understand the way we got here and what can be done? Feminist thinkers contend that these developments cannot be comprehended, let alone reversed, without an understanding of gender and its part in the development of the forms of knowledge and power integral to these dilemmas. Gender, masculine and feminine, must be at the center of discussions about the most general issues of our time, not invoked only in discussions of the condition of women. In this book Sally Hacker contributes to this ongoing feminist effort to make gendered the terms in which we think about today's human condition.

Hacker poses a series of questions, each illuminating in some way the problem of how human creativity has been turned back on itself as a destructive force. How are the pleasures of making things work (technology) turned into processes of domination? Are there links between gender and military institutions, and are both linked to the form technology takes in our society? Does eroticism have something to do with engineering? How can human life, including work life, be organized as more egalitarian and more humane? And can feminism help us with the answers?

Pleasure, Power, and Technology is, in addition to a discussion of these issues, an account of a sociological life and of the feminist-sociological knowledge that life has produced. A sociological life is one in which the dichtomy, characteristic of our times, between work and life is dissolved, as the sociologist uses the discipline to understand her own experience and, reciprocally, in a self-reflective process, uses her life to inform and shape what she does as a sociologist. Setting her research within its own historical and intellectual circumstances, she tells us why she asked her sociological questions, and how she went about, often in unorthodox ways, extracting answers from difficult social terrain. Questions that need to be answered are rooted in the dilemmas of contending with an unjust, oppressive society. The sought-after answers, she hopes, will provide some practical ideas about what to do, as well as the pleasures inherent in being able to pose a question and find ways to answer it.

This stance toward doing sociology is, I believe, much more often found among those who hope to change the world than among those who are content to make a career amid things as they are. For the satisfied or the timid, few openly articulated connections may exist between the imperatives of their own experience and the questions that inform their research. Of course, this is not only a matter of relative satisfaction and timidity, but one of the proper aims and methods of sociology. The persistent notion that what sociologists are doing is building a science somewhat analogous to physics, albeit an outmoded physics, tends to encourage a disjuncture between life and work. Research methods in this tradition seek to promote objectivity by arguing the necessity for such a separation; the values, interests, and subjectivity of the investigator have no place in science. Such an approach, as many others have argued, conceals behind a myth of objectivity the fact that knowledge is socially produced by humans whose social locations inevitably produce a point of view that informs their work. Much of the work in this tradition has a fault perhaps as serious as the error of living with an illusion—it lacks excitement, often because methodological questions become more important than substantive ones.

Better—more informative and theoretically interesting—sociology comes, I believe, when questions are asked, not because they can be answered using a particular method, but because the answers make a difference. That is the kind of sociology Sally Hacker did. She was not satisfied or timid, and the account of the connections between her research and her life as an activist is a fascinating, and too rare, piece of writing. Without polemic, she stands firmly for a sociology that contributes to change, candidly showing how her emerging political intent informed her changing research focus. Growing feminist and radical-democratic concerns helped to formulate the issues she addressed, as, beginning in the 1960s, she and her friends "fairly burst with a desire for a new society" and "settled on a yeasty blend of social anarchism and feminism" to help guide their experiments with communal and cooperative living and working. This theme, how we can organize our lives in more feminist-egalitarian ways, runs through Hacker's work, emerging as the major question in her last study of the cooperative Basque community, Mondragon.

Gender inequality and the impact of technology on power imbalances between the sexes are part of the problem of achieving more communal and humane forms of social life. For Sally, complex webs of experience, beginning with a childhood fascination with the technics of backyard Tarzan ropes, swings, and teeter-totters, led to a feeling for the pleasures of work and technology and a deep curiosity about how work becomes alienated and technology an instrument for creating and maintaining inequality and oppression. Technology seemed to take this ominous role in the explanation of the disappointing outcome of efforts in the early 1970s to achieve affirmative action for women and minorities at AT&T. Sally Hacker was, for years, chairperson of the National Organization for Women's AT&T task force, which achieved a stunning victory in forcing this huge company to institute measures to integrate women and minorities into formerly white male jobs. As she details in her study of this victory, "the gains we made through affirmative action were wiped out by jobs lost to automation."

On the trail of an explanation for this victory turned defeat, she found that managers rather than technology were responsible, and that most high-level managers were engineers, leading to subsequent studies of engineers and their education, particularly how they learn to see and treat other human beings as only elements in a system. At the same time, she continued her active participation in the women's movement and her active exploration of forms of feminist theory, liberal, socialist, radical, and anarchic. Studying engineers could produce knowledge that feminists needed to understand the pervasive organization of male domination. The next steps of the search led to the military, its central involvement in technology and the development of engineering, and the nature of the military as a gendered institution. Continuing involvement in feminist issues in the 1980s helped to raise again the question of pleasure, and also sexuality, and how discipline and hierarchy integral to the organization of male-dominated technology and military structures shape and use the erotic component of human life. Finally the thread leads back to the problem of future—how can we do it better? Are there examples of social life in which work is an expression of creativity, and women are not oppressed, the erotic is not deformed, and pleasure marks daily life?

Research experiences are lived experiences that, as much as political commitments and daily happenings, act back upon the researcher's sense of the problematic. Working with statistical analyses of data gathered by others distances the researcher from the living source of the data, other people, and narrows the range of questions that can be explored. Sally Hacker began, in the AT&T study, with statistical analysis, but her questions more and more demanded additional approaches to data gathering. She used a wide array of methods, from archival research to interviews and questionnaires to various forms of participant observation. In her participant observation, life and work emerged most clearly. She sat in classrooms to study engineering education and finally became a student herself in order to understand what happens to consciousness of relationships and material reality in the course of a person's transformation into an engineer. Thus, her own subjective processes became part of the material she analyzed. To study the fate of women in the lower depths of engineering and new technology, she took a leave without pay to try to get a job in computer manufacture and, failing, got to experience unemployment and life on the economic margins in a large industrial city.

In these and other ways this sociological life is enmeshed in the objects of its study, while staying close to its origins in working-class, small-town, midwestern U.S.A., and making the connections between those origins and increasingly broad questions of work, technology, and gender. This is an unusual and, as Sally would say, "yeasty" mix for a sociologist. Most of us don't manage to stay so close to our material, to our commitments, or to our roots. And this mix contributes to the emerging feminist transformation of critical understandings of industrial capitalism.

Feminist scholarship is moving from a focus on questions about women's disadvantage and difference to placing those questions within a broader problematic of the gendering of all social structures and processes. This means a move from an emphasis on women's work, the family, and sex-role socialization to include the organization of and symbolic representation of gender in the emergence and present functioning of male-dominated locations of power, such as the military and the capitalist economy. It also means a renewed emphasis, long existing in some radical feminist writing, on trying to understand masculinity and how it is implicated in the structure of power and domination.

This new scholarship, taking many different lines of investigation, is producing a reinterpretation of human society and of the history of the Western world. Sally Hacker's work is part of this development, contributing importantly to this analysis, particularly in connecting technology to gender and the organization of male-dominated, institutionalized power.

Gender, technology, and power are linked in many ways. Sally Hacker was one of the first to show that such a linkage appears often in the process of implementing technological change. Her study of AT&T demonstrated how management used gender as a tool to facilitate the introduction of new technology; by integrating women into male jobs scheduled for elimination, the process could be made easier, they thought, as women's high turnover rates would allow reduction of the work force without complaint. Subsequent work by many others continues to show, in varying patterns,

how technological change is almost always gender differentiated, reproducing women's disadvantage even in the
process of trying to ameliorate it, as in the AT&T case.

Technology, gender, and power are also linked through
gendered definitions and distributions of skill; this is another
understanding to which Sally Hacker's work contributes. For
example, her research on engineering education shows how
images of gender are involved in the making of the
engineer's skills and how the exclusion of women is part of
the process of creating these skills as masculine. Such ideas
have an affinity with the work of Cynthia Cockburn (1983,
1985), who describes in a number of studies how masculinity
becomes identified with skill and technology in a process
that defines the feminine as unskilled and inept with
technology. The deadly combination of male control of
technology—masculine gender identity—and male power
keeps women in their place. The detailed unraveling of how
this deadly combination works is integral to our emergent
new theory of a gendered industrial capitalism.

The role of masculine eroticism in oppressive power, as
expressed through increasingly sophisticated technology, is
another essential part of this emergent theory. This is not an
argument that men are evil, but rather the puzzle, as Hacker
puts it, of trying to comprehend "how men are persuaded to
give over autonomy, and come to value a narrow technical
rationality rather than reason, to accept as normal and right
the contemporary shape of relationships, sexuality and
eroticism, technology and work. . . . Who in their right
mind would give up so much for so little privilege over others
and why" Further, who benefits, and how? Part of the answer
Hacker gives to the first question is that the work of
engineering is exhilarating, and that eroticism is at the core
of the exhilaration. But control and discipline, linked to the
military-industrial roots of engineering, are also involved,
which contributes to the eroticization of domination and the
conviction that rationality demands treating people as
things. Thus, Hacker ties the feminist discussion of
eroticism, domination, and the subordination of women to
the development of a technology that is a central aspect of
core institutions, the economy, and the military.

Hacker's work enriches another important, and related, part of the reinterpretation of Western society that feminist scholars are developing. This is the feminist critique of science, such as that of Hilary Rose (1983), who argues, following earlier writers such as Carolyn Merchant (1980), that a distorted, masculine science tied to capitalist accumulation processes and militarism is threatening human life. Hacker's work on the history of engineering and mathematics education describes how this education was shaped on the West Point military model, emphasizing a rigid discipline and control that became part of rational masculinity. With her husband, military historian Barton Hacker, she explored gender in the history of the military, filling in other important pieces of the puzzle about how we got to such a perilous situation; a different picture of the development of capitalism and its present contradictions begins to emerge as the importance of gender and the military become more evident.

Like Rose, Hacker refuses to reject science and technology and tries to imagine their transformation instead. Some have turned to science fiction and utopian writing for images of the future; Sally Hacker traveled to Mondragon to look at the most famous cooperative community in the Western world. The second part of the book is devoted to her study of Mondragon. The results are not encouraging. Gender relations are traditional in Mondragon, although co-op women are somewhat better off than similar women in nearby communities. In Mondragon, as elsewhere, patriarchal power is supported by a mostly male monopoly over technical knowledge. As co-op industry becomes more involved in international markets, new technology and its accompanying ideology of the engineer and the hierarchical organization of work are being uncritically accepted. It seems that participative democracy in production will be undermined without an understanding that hierarchy and dominance are built into the technology in the interests of a masculine military-industrial hegemony.

Thus, from diverse directions, the notion that gender and sexuality are implicated not only in the subordination of women, but in the fundamental constitution of our societies, not only in a separate sphere of reproduction, but in the economy and polity, is crowding against the old conceptions of gender-neutral structures and processes. This is, of course, not a new idea for feminists, and many in the second wave of feminism have been saying it for some time; the knowledge that the personal is political leads to the knowledge that gender pervades social process. What is different now is the research, such as Sally Hacker has done, that begins to show in concrete detail how this happens, revealing connections, such as that between eroticism and technology, that we must comprehend if we are to understand the terrible attractions of the ties that oppress. We are tied to, collude in, rational systems of technical control, her work suggests, not only by material interests, force, and ideology, but because they also provide pleasure.

But pleasure can be turned around in the interest of social change. People have to get together to change things, Sally Hacker reminds us. This is serious business, but if there isn't a little fun in being together, a little kick out of being contentious, not much will happen. Pleasure does not have to be perverted as an instrument of dominance. There are oppositional models, and this sociological life shows that they exist.

JOAN ACKER

INTRODUCTION

In the midst of movements for women's rights, civil rights, and peace, I worked with telephone workers to help women and minorities get a better deal. We won back pay. We won access to higher-level and nontraditional jobs for women and minorities. As it turned out, the gains made through affirmative action were wiped out by jobs lost to automation. And where we had been successful opening craft jobs for women, we found we had helped the company replace more costly with less expensive workers, as craft work became computer-related clerical work. What's more, management found less resistance to full automation if the redundant workers were women.

These outcomes and others affecting women—elimination of jobs where minority women cluster, for example, 35,000 clerical and office jobs in three years—were closely related to massive technological changes in telecommunications. These changes themselves were influenced by needs of military as well as economic institutions. So we won; more women moved into craft work and some into management. At the same time, we lost; fewer women were employed.

It became a mystery, a whodunnit of industrial change. We had to find some answers. The first answer—technology did it—was too simple but partially correct, and thus the more treacherous. One could sigh, sit back, and wait to see what "it" would do next. "It" was powerful, inexorable, overwhelming. And "it" was bad.

This view of women as victims of technology was all well and good—group solidarity through pissing and moaning. The trouble was twofold: such a view gave us no purchase on what to do next, and, besides, I liked "technology." I was fascinated by the human care and wit and cleverness we could express through it.

In the jargon of my field, sociology, we are "taking technology as the independent variable"—the thing that caused other things to happen as in the harvester eliminated farm work, or the washer-dryer made laundry a women-only job, or computers eliminated the need for teachers. We had new questions. Who "caused" technology? It doesn't happen all by itself. Who designed and built harvesters, why those kinds of harvesters, and on whose money? Then we learned to see the importance that lay not in cause or effect alone, but in the constant interaction between technology and society in everyday life, and the history of these interactions.

This book first describes the pleasures of growing up with technology as a natural part of life, then suggests that we have gendered that pleasure, affecting both social structure and the shape of technology. Technology involves a strong sensual and erotic dimension. Whoever captures and defines erotic energy, a source of great social power, has more than an edge on the rest. This book explores how technology has been captured in the past, and finds that gendering limits people's ability to use their energies creatively, even in a cooperative workplace. As a result, the book argues that freeing technology from its gender-bound state is part of the liberation of our ways of living and thinking—part of returning the power of technology to the members of a democratic society.

The first chapter suggests that technology has been masculinized and controlled by an elite for thousands of years, chiefly by and through military institutions and their technical arm, engineering. It explains a few terms, gives some examples, and reveals a lot about the underlying set of experiences and feelings that influence action and theory as presented here.

Chapter 2 describes the ways women and people of color were affected differently, or at different times, by technological change. I found that in practice different feminist actions and theoretical perspectives had advantages and disadvantages, as we asked, Why and who created the technologies we have, and who benefited at whose expense? I explore the way various actions and perspectives influenced each other. In Chapter 2, liberal, socialist, and radical feminism; later, perspectives of the social constructionist, historian, and anarchafeminist—a social anarchism centered on feminist goals.

At the end of Chapter 2, I describe how some managers with engineering backgrounds organized work, designed the industrial systems, the administrative apparatuses; what they thought about women, workers, minorities; how their jokes reveal a peculiar concern with the body and its functions. At times, they designed work with race and gender in mind. I became fascinated to know how they justified what they did, and how they got to sleep at night. Chapter 3 carries on this tale of the technologists. I describe a couple of years I spent at MIT, researching the culture and ideology of engineering, where I thought the linkages among industry, technology, and social hierarchy might be greatest. I explore beliefs and notions about women, sensual pleasure, and nature among this elite engineering faculty. It seemed that the erotic component obvious in writing, thinking, and practicing technology had in this institution taken a strange turn—not only a masculinized technology, but one preoccupied with itself. Feminine components of the technological process— women and nature, for example—were simultaneously idealized, teased, ignored, and sharply controlled.

I began, then, to wonder about ordinary everyday engineers and the institutions that produced them. I had learned that their jobs and work processes, like those of telephone workers, are also now becoming routine, and they compete with cheaper technical help to work with the new computer-related design equipment. I wanted to know how it felt to become an engineer, what was in it for them. Most would not likely become corporate executives of multi-nationals, but would staff government and corporate administrations, or wind up in sales. I began to suspect the price some men paid for the promise of high salary and prestigious work was giving up reciprocal erotic relations with women. The cost to women was giving up themselves and becoming one of the guys.

In Chapter 3, the whodunnit approach—technology, capitalism, the military, and the state—gives way, then, to ethnographic research in the engineering classroom of a large western land-grant university. I became an engineering student to see how it felt. Parts of it were exciting and enjoyable; some of it was grim. I began to realize how we participate in and thus support, hierarchical processes by taking part; what becomes appealing, how we give in and get bought out, but also how we resist.

Resistance works better if you know some of the history behind what you are resisting. And so in Chapter 4 I search for how things got to be the way they are in engineering education. Engineering is the technical branch of the military, and engineering education often serves to maintain gender stratification during periods of rapid change. Engineers are the radicals of our time, changing the physical and social world piecemeal, often without a thought for the whole. This chapter explores the roots of engineering and technical culture in military institutions, and what that means for the organization of work, technology, and eroticism. Military institutions—here focused on technical education—shape the everyday lives not only of their own people, but also of other men and women, directly or indirectly, from establishing patterns for the administration of the labor process to the structure of appropriate desire.

We go in fits and starts, creating new and more democratic forms, then undermining them. Truly it is the effort that counts. Today, there are many fruitful contradictions between the organization of technology and a fully participatory society. One such contradiction comes with women's increasing numbers in engineering and the military. Another is cooperative, "democratic" workplaces, which are still gender stratified and use a machine and social technology that demands hierarchical organization. I turn to these and other issues in Chapter 5.

Technology, including the organization of work, is currently authoritarian in its structure and ideology. Much of the pattern of inequality rests on gender stratification, among and between men and women. People chafe under domination. Some of us resist patterns of hierarchy as they are created, but sometimes we forget how. Somebody is stealing our resistance stories, or, more likely, eroding the situations for their telling. How might we organize our societies for more participatory democracy, differently from the patterns described in Part I? What does it take? We are here concerned with how gender can be diffused and technology redesigned to reflect and create cooperation rather than domination and exploitation.

There is no nonpatriarchal industrial society from which to draw inspiration, no society unimplicated in military institutions, the central patriarchal institutions of today. Within such societies, however, alternative social forms continually emerge. Some last; all leave a trace. Our participation in creating them and working and playing in them is more important than their permanence. They offer the means of participatory democracy. The ends may never fully be achieved, as revolution is continuous.

In Part II, I explore cooperative alternatives for one institution—the workplace. In a fully democratic and participatory workplace, we should expect to find better relations among gender, race, and technology. We shall see. In the United States and elsewhere, there is currently a relatively strong wave of cooperativism. These movements represent action along a spectrum from suggestion box and team production or employee stock ownership plans to workplaces fully owned and managed by workers who decide what to produce and how, and where the profits should go. But workplaces do not function in isolation. So we explore implications for other institutions such as family, church, leisure. Ultimately, I will suggest that significant changes in these must accompany a general degendering and a redefinition of eroticism around equal and reciprocal relations between and among men and women. Our resistance to concentrations of power takes many forms. It can be at times individual, intellectual, literary, spiritual. But it must also be collective and political, giving priority to self-articulated needs of working—waged and unwaged—women.

Industrial cooperative work has a history as long as that of industrial society itself. And women have been involved in the making of it since the beginning. Chapter 5 traces part of British and U.S. history, which is still inaccurately white and male. The opportunities for students of women's studies to follow the lives of women in this history, to tell us some stories, are many.

Chapter 5 begins on the historical note of Chapter 4, but traces a brief history of cooperativism rather than the history of military institutions. It finishes with a description of one of the most successful contemporary industrial cooperatives, the Mondragon system of worker-owned and -managed production cooperatives in Euskadi, Basque Country, in northern Spain. It is the most often studied system, and rightly so. We need to understand how the models are structured, and how they work. But the literature on Mondragon and other cooperatives ignores gender. Gender is the crucial ingredient to bring participatory technology and democracy to the fore.

Chapter 6 introduces the concept of gender, analyzes the condition of women in the Mondragon system, and finds it to be more similar than not to women's position in capitalist or socialist workplaces. This is true despite the egalitarian nature of Basque culture and the absence of military institutions except for a semiautonomous state and police. The cooperatives maintain contradictory approaches to both gender and technology rooted in patriarchal institutions of the past. This chapter discusses links among work, family, past military influence, and church, and how the important institutions of leisure bear on the process of democracy.

Chapter 7 summarizes the organization of gender and technology. It explores differences between authoritarian and cooperative workplaces, and makes some suggestions for cooperative society, eliminating gender and liberating eroticism. This and Chapter 8 suggest collective action among working women, in these cases around the organization of technology, through a politics of linkages with others (Gunn 1984). I conclude with arguments for tolerance of differences among those of us who resist current forms of authority, and a strong suggestion for more public and local action toward that goal.

PART I

Gender, Technology, and Work: Thought and Action

CHAPTER 1

Tools of Pleasure
and Power

My older sister Sue and I helped some, but mostly squatted and watched, as Dad dug the foot-deep hole, filled it with cement, and eased the six-foot piece of plumbing pipe upright in the mix. When it set, he fastened an elbow joint to the pipe's top. It held the horizontal bar whose other end lodged firmly into the old maple. He made two trapezes and a swing from lengths of chain, small pipes, and a slab of wood, and hung them from the bar. The dozen or so kids in the backyard tribe gathered to see what he would do next. A lower horizontal bar off to the right supported the teeter-totter, a long, flat board nailed to iron circles the bar ran through. Then came the Tarzan rope, which swung from the maple's largest limb, with a great knot at the bottom for a

Off to the left of the tree, another bar supported the two-seater ferris wheel. This bar ran through the middle of two ten-foot boards, held apart by a couple of two-foot iron pipes at either end. Dad hung a small swing seat on chains from each pipe. One person slid into the bottom seat; another climbed the latter to the platform built for this purpose, and (very carefully) got into the top seat. Thus balanced, each rider pumped it like a swing—back and up, then over the top and down again, as slow or as fast as we wanted. The pace of this muscle-powered machine was determined by mutual delight, or through a lot of hollering, threats, negotiating, or foot dragging when all else failed. Sometimes some of the boys dumped each other out on their heads, then we kicked them out for a day.

My favorite was the trolley. Dad wrapped a cable high up around the old maple, above the platform, and winched it tightly around the other tree next to the house. He bolted the trolley to a pulley that ran along the cable. The trolley itself was an upside-down T. We drew it up to the platform with a length of twine, held onto the upright, climbed on, lifted off, and flew down the cable, angled so you could bash into the tree at the other end of the yard with just the right amount of force. Maximal excitement, minimal damage, although over the years, the maple near the house showed a shiny barkless circle from the battering by small feet.

In some ten years, there were only three injuries as I recall. Ruth Ann broke her wrist on the ferris wheel, getting into the top seat before the bottom was loaded. I chipped a front tooth on the trapeze bar from standing too close while I pushed Nicky. And Virginia, who liked to let the Tarzan rope swing down its pendulum arc until you could barely jump for it from the top of the platform, missed and plowed up several feet of southern Illinois soil with her chin; lost no teeth, broke no bones.

Sue and her friends organized a carnival at one or two cents a ride, complete with halloween horror shows in the basement. We sold half a carton of what we thought was dad's homemade root beer for a nickel each before the discovery we'd grabbed the wrong box and were selling the homemade real stuff. All proceeds from the carnival were divided evenly among those who worked. In this one-shot venture, it never occurred to us to consider the ownership of the means of pleasure in this distribution process.

Other actions grew from our collective and individual interest in pleasure. All were not successful. Our town had no swimming pool. Once a month or so, Mom and Dad loaded the old Graham with kids and drove ten miles to the next town for a swim. One summer we learned that some of the townsmen, Dad included, planned a small airport, some said to enhance economic development. The backyard kids demonstrated through the three blocks of downtown, beating pans and lids, carrying signs demanding a swimming pool first. We got an airport.

Mom was the first of a farm family, a family with many children but few acres, to move into town and take a job in the Kodak shop. Sue and I once found a purple velvet fringed and sequined dress in the back of her closet. Much to

4

our surprise, we learned this fairly staid couple had a past. In the days of flappers, speakeasies, and big bands, they tooled around the countryside on a two-chain-driven Indian motocycle, or in an old Model T, held parties in the backyard and picnics in the country. They followed the stories of Mother Jones, whose tomb is ten miles away in Mt. Olive, with some interest.

Mom—solid, strong, and fun-loving—managed the backyard with a firm hand but usually let us solve our own problems. She fixed lemonade or cocoa depending on the season, cleaned and labeled a small drinking can for each of us, and lined the tins up on the sill outside the kitchen window. Now homemaker, wife, and mother, yet she encouraged an exuberant equality among the children, discouraged gender differentiation with a cold look or a sharp word. She admonished: "Be fair!" "Take turns!" and "No running that trolley between 2:00 and 4:00 p.m.!" (Dad worked as a clerk in the post office starting at 4:00 p.m., and napped afternoons.) She enjoyed the backyard most, I think. Dad liked to make her laugh, and it was a kick.

Technology is defined as the organization of material and energy to accomplish work. Raising children is work, and surely the social and machine technics of the backyard helped accomplish it. Work has bad press these days, and for good reason. Some oppose it to leisure. But technology is strongly related to pleasure. It has its sensual and erotic dimensions, one of the themes of this book. Technology is, however, also gendered and thus reflects differences in power between men and women. The liberation of technology, work, and pleasure in general requires the elimination or diffusion of gender. Structured differences in power between men and women are the stuff of gender, from which it emerges, and which gender helps maintain (de Lauretis 1987). Work also can be a pleasure. Rather than the onerous tasks men dream of automating, work can be thought of as an opportunity to express ourselves most fully. I take Marx's more hopeful definition as a goal, that work can be an expression of human creativity and a source of freedom (Street 1983). When I talk about technology and work, I'm thinking about the backyard.

5

Some Terms and Definitions

Most of us do not live and work consistently within a fully developed theoretical framework. In fact, most of us hold some notions that are quite contradictory to other notions we believe just as strongly. Sometimes we say one thing in theory and do another in practice. This is perhaps unavoidable. But contradictions are not randomly distributed through social life, nor are they of equal severity. They appear today with striking force in the three areas of concern I address—gender, technology, and cooperativism. My hope is that the stories in this book will help clarify some of the contradictions within and between our theory and practice. As Cynthia Cockburn (1983) puts it in her analysis of gender and the printing trades, we are limited by our social positions and characteristics. Each makes conflicting demands on our thoughts and feelings and alliances, such as traditional notions of gender and strong beliefs in equality of opportunity. These contradictions are painful. They continually demand new decisions to be made, alliances be maintained or ended, sides taken, new syntheses discovered.

> Such elaborations of paradox and confusion are painstaking and often painful. But it is precisely out of the process of bringing such contradictions to consciousness and facing up to illogicality or inconsistency, that a person takes a grip on his or her own fate. Politically it is of vital importance that we understand how we change. (Cockburn 1983:13)

First, a brief explication of terms. We can think of a social *theory* as an explanation, on a fairly general level, of why things happen as they do. Perhaps a man joins an office or workplace and advances faster than a woman who helped train him, or women with more education and training than he. Black or Hispanic women do not move up as rapidly as do Anglo women. Or, you do not see as many women over 45 in high-level positions as you do men. Perhaps among men or women, those who have passed courses in calculus, have a degree in engineering, or have had military experience are considered the best people for upper-level management positions. Or, the workplace structure is a very tall pyramid: Those at the top work with their minds and make broad-ranging decisions; those at the bottom work with their hands at repetitive tasks, or do lots of "face work" to please other people. Some people, firms, industries, and countries can't find the resources they need for social projects, while others can. How did things get that way? How do we explain these patterns? Who benefits? And at whose expense?

There are other patterns in social behavior. Many women have similar complaints about the men they date, with whom they live or work, or merely pass in the streets. People "gender" the social and physical world (Mother Nature), thinking some things are masculine, some are feminine. We gender most experience, from tools and their use to erotic styles. Women everywhere still do most of the housework and child care. Concerns about sexuality and family are considered private and personal, rarely analyzed along with technology and work. The stories we tell to explain these patterns are nascent social theories.

Technology is not simply machines. Technology can be defined as the organization of materials and energy to accomplish work. Work is a preparation, a making, a shaping, something upon which labor is expended. The area of leisure studies indicates how difficult it can become to draw the line between work and leisure. We most often think of military and industrial technology, but we can also think of technologies of child care or housework, leisure or education. The important point is that technology is both mechanical and social.

Machines and systems are designed, developed, and applied by people. They do not fall from the sky. They are designed and used with a great deal of passion (Levy 1984; Keller 1985; Kidder 1981). Technology also comprises highly complex systems of social relations. So, by the term *technology*, I mean the machines and the social relations (Rothschild 1983; Noble 1984).

Most often we think of the social relations of production as the way institutions and people arrange for and accomplish work. Some of those social relations are sensuous—appealing to or derived from the senses. This is a special aspect of technology. Some relations are also sensual, pleasurable in a more specific way, appealing to sexual desire in particular. Later, I explore the relationship between technology and *eroticism*, the erotic being that which is designed to arouse sexual desire.

I use *gender* to mean the set of beliefs and expectations considered appropriate to males or females.

Generally, we react against injustice when we see it, and often try to do something about it. Sometimes we simply pursue our own personal goals within the system. But the system rests firmly on its patriarchal base. This path, then, does little to change the organization of gender, technology, or work that constrains our lives. At other, better times, we join together to create new social forms.

. This book addresses the relationships among gender, technology, and work, at a time when major social changes appear imminent in all three. Usually these changes occur within the dominant patriarchal framework of civilized societies, but there are always such counter tendencies as feminism, appropriate technology and environmental movements, and the movement for democratic workplaces and communities. Only in the most comprehensive movements for social change do we find these tendencies combined. A second theme of this book is that of the relationships between military institutions and gender, technology, and work. Military institutions and their technical arm, engineering, are among the foremost yet most often overlooked patriarchal institutions. They provide us with some of the first instances of structured gender hierarchy, and provide hierarchical models for the organization of technology and work. Military institutions have a beginning, as discussed in Chapter 4. This makes it easier to imagine life without them.

A Brief Overview of
the History of Technology

Lewis Mumford, eminent historian and ace storyteller, captures images of creativity and freedom in his accounts of

8

the human experience with technology and work. According to Mumford (1967–1970), tool-making is less central to our nature than symbol-making, linguistic symbols in particular. The nonmaterial parts of our culture enhanced our technology more than the reverse. Our most important tool, Mumford (1972) says, is our "own mind-activated body," with "its extraordinary lability and plasticity" (p. 78), allowing us to use the environment and our own inner resources so effectively. Life-enhancing cultural work such as song and ritual, dance and play are more important than merely utilitarian manual work, which is but a piece of our biotechnics, our total equipment for living.

Mumford's radical proposal is that our need for a common symbolic culture, our need to shape and channel the "tumultuous energy of our psycho-social expressive capacity," had more to do with technological transformations than did our need to increase the food supply or otherwise control the forces of nature. "Foraging called less for tools than for sharp observation . . . wide experimental sampling . . . and a shrewd interpretation of the effects . . . upon the human organism" (1972:80). Taste and formal beauty, he notes—color and form of flower, perfume, texture and spiciness—along with nutrition, played their role in horticultural discoveries. The Neolithic domestication of plants and animals owed much

> to an intense subjective concentration of sexuality in all its manifestations. . . . Plant selection, hybridization, fertilization, manuring, seeding, castration were the products of an imaginative cultivation of sexuality, whose first evidence one finds tens of thousands of years earlier. . . . The Neolithic garden, like gardens in many simpler cultures today, was probably a mixture of food plants, dye plants, medicinals, and ornamentals—all treated as equally essential for life. (1972:81)

Even the classic concept of technics did not distinguish as we do today "between industrial production and art, . . . one side respecting objective conditions and functions, the other responding to subjective needs and expressing sharable feelings and meanings" (1972:80).

Over the centuries, Neolithic horticultural societies gave

way to agricultural; children became economically and politically useful, and it became women's role to produce them. In some societies, for reasons both economic and political, wives began to settle near their husband's families, and the passing on of names and things was reckoned through fathers rather than through mothers. There, with men living near their kin, and women the relative outsiders, fraternal interest groups emerged. These men's groups strengthened their solidarity through reproductive rituals such as circumcision, and enhanced control over women and children as resources through rituals of marriage and childbirth (Paige and Paige 1981).

In contrast to more egalitarian prestate societies, fraternal interest groups became small bands of soldiers, men living together and largely living off the work of women, children, and older folk who provided their food and comfort (Weber 1968). Unlike "warrior," a tribal member who sometimes fought, "soldier" in time became a full-time role. It is our thesis (Hacker and Hacker 1987) that these military bands illustrate the beginnings of armies and other military institutions characterizing patriarchal societies, such as states and industries with the primary purpose of providing for equipment, weapons, and fortifications. Military institutions demand societies organized for their support. Separate, differentiated from society in general, military institutions emerged some 5000 years ago. They arose with, and depended upon, women's structured subordination to men via the military. One might say the military is the oldest industry and soldiering the oldest profession. Strong bonds and behavior appropriate for hierarchical, unequal relations between and among men and women develop—the eroticism of power and powerlessness. The social energy of eroticism is thus caught, and shapes institutions, labor processes, the organization of work and of technology. Mumford refers to this hierarchical organization as "authoritarian technics," as opposed to the life-centered "biotechnics" of the Neolithic era.

One might rather argue such a prominence for religious roles and institutions rather than for military. Indeed, the structure of these patriarchal societies both reflected and was reflected in their religions. Mumford describes not only the transformation to hierarchical state societies, but the accompanying, worldwide transformation to patriarchal religions, such as that honoring "Atum Re, the Sun God, who characteristically created the world out of his own semen without female cooperation" (Mumford 1972:81). The reigning deity of the dominant religion in our own culture was modest by comparison, using merely clay.

No institution, including military, is monolithic. Interaction between military and society produces change in each. Our argument for the exceptionally powerful influence of military institutions on gender, technology, and work in all civilized societies, however, is linked to the pervasive influence of military discipline and hierarchical structure on the organization of work, the labor process, the family, and all other major social institutions. As Weber (1968) put it, "Military discipline gives birth to all discipline. . . . It has always in some way affected the structure of the state, the economy, and possibly the family" (pp. 1153, 1155). A few older men with positions of power and authority commanded a hierarchical organization of people disciplined for performance of specialized pieces of a whole project. Engineering was also a military project, the term *civil engineering* coined in the eighteenth century to distinguish it from more typically military pursuits (B. Hacker 1986). The first engineering schools, as was West Point, were military academies. Graduates often reshaped workplaces after these military institutions. Work became a burden in patriarchal societies, hierarchical rather than cooperative, a single task separate from other biological and social activities. The ancient dreams of power and omnipotence, the elimination of work, says Mumford, are with us still.

It remained for feminists to suggest—and then, through women's studies scholars in literature, history, and anthropology, to explicate—women's active agency in technological transformation (Daly 1973; Boulding 1976; Stone 1976; Ortner 1972; Griffin 1978; Bernard 1981; Starhawk 1982; Stanley 1983; Lerner 1986). It is surprising, however, that so little feminist attention is directed toward military institutions. We puzzle over the "takeover," the "worldwide subordination of women," the "creation of patriarchy." Yet we rarely analyze military institutions, primary models of patriarchal forms of social organization, which were most salient in these processes.

Thus, military institutions supported gender hierarchy, in times of challenge to it, in the first state societies. During the Middle Ages, state and military once again guided relations among gender, technology, and work; as the size of government, and the extent of laws governing work increased, women were excluded from the crafts (Cockburn 1985; Hanawalt 1986); militarization excluded most from monasteries and education (Noble forthcoming). Military institutions are complex, and they interact with civilian institutions such as family, schools, church, and industry in many ways; the line is thin at best. Military institutions can at once create and react to a new technology. The reaction is sometimes enthusiastic, sometimes resistant to change, and depends on location within the systems and subsystems of the military.

Most often, however, military institutions initiate gender inequality. A few examples include the exclusion of camp followers from early modern armies (B. Hacker 1981), the parallel growth of military and prostitution both in the United States (Weeks 1986) and in other countries (Heyzer 1986:59, Neumann 1978–1979:23), the definition of craft and engineering work as masculine within the military, and the rigid division of labor according to gender at the workplace (Hacker and Hacker 1987). Finally, consider the influence on subordination emerging from and entering the everyday lives of women as soldiers, nurses, wives, and clerical workers in military institutions (Enloe 1983). In Chapter 4, I explore further the relationships among military, institutions, engineering, technology, and other aspects of the labor process, and how these institutions help gender the structure of pleasure.

Military institutions long predate capitalism, which adds yet another dimension to men's exploitation and oppression of each other, of women as a class (Acker 1980), and, to a lesser extent, some women's exploitation and oppression of others as well (Glazer 1984). For some fifty centuries or

12

more, patriarchal institutions have shaped sexuality, technology, and work. In the several million years of human experience, this is not so long a period of time, though certainly it is more than enough. All along, as they could, some women, men, and children have resisted or diverted these institutional demands, which benefit the few at the expense of the many. We have created various private worlds in the interstices of these institutions. We have sometimes created revolutionary social and cultural movements toward societies where work is that expression of human creativity and source of freedom of which Marx wrote.

Oppositional Forms of Social Organization

This book contrasts the typical organization of work in bureaucractic, industrial societies with worker-owned and -controlled cooperative workplaces. Some argue that cooperatives are in themselves revolutionary, others that cooperatives are a prerevolutionary social form of human organization. Their philosophical and practical roots are grounded in the traditions of social anarchism (Ferguson 1984; Rothschild and Whitt 1986; Lindenfeld 1986).

Social anarchism does not represent the tyranny of structurelessness observed by Jo Freeman (1975:119–129), where informal yet not less structured power relations are denied or ignored. Social anarchism (as opposed to right-wing or individual anarchism) is densely structured to diffuse such concentrations of power while encouraging individuality in community context. Social anarchists reach backward in time and across cultures for knowledge of societies governing themelves by custom or consensus, without state, military, or bureaucratic-legal institutions (Black 1976). They offer models for the present and for the future of industrial society as in Bookchin's *Post-Scarcity Anarchism* (1971), which deals with issues of production, distribution, and political organization in today's industrial countries; as in Quaker practice, which emphasizes decisions based on consensus and opposes hierarchy; or as in the radical proposals of Basques and others for countries without states, for a "Federation of European Cultures." Large-scale social anarchist movements in modern societies, however, such as those in Spain in the 1930s, were not necessarily feminist and seldom made significant gains for women (Kornegger 1975). But it is only in these left-libertarian or utopian socialist movements where issues of sexuality and women's experience have, at times, shared center stage (Benenson 1984; Phillips 1983). The latest wave of cooperativism in the United States expresses once more the irrepressible desire and human capacity for democratic self-governance.

Almost 20 years ago in Iowa, some 30 to 40 of us fairly burst with a desire for a new society. We read Marx, Mao, Lenin, Malatesta, and Firestone, among others, picking and choosing as we went. We settled on a yeasty blend of social anarchism and feminism. We learned to share skills, rotate the various tasks necessary to keep households, meetings, and organizations running, made decisions by consensus more often than not, learned to criticize ourselves and others in as near a constructive way as we could. We paid attention to gender differences in technical skills. In general, it is men who possess tools and technical competence, "an extension of the physical domination of women by men . . . [which has] extensive effects in differential earnings and social authority" (Cockburn 1985:7–8).

In the collectives, many of us had to learn as children do, slowly and clumsily, how to use tools. We learned related habits, too, such as cleaning and replacing tools when we finished with them. We learned to buy tools, a particularly difficult lesson for some of us. It was even harder to keep them in hand. At a regional meeting, a college professor took a hammer from the hand of a young woman at work. He wanted to help finish the job more quickly and efficiently, he explained at the meeting called to discuss the issue. We talked about the differences between long- and short-term efficiency.

Trying to work things out, we talked a strange and sometimes awkward language, about "deprivatizing our possessive relationships" and the like. When Jacob was born to one of us (who pointed out to the many she was the only person doing childcare, while the rest of us did revolution), we talked about deprivatizing our possessive biological relations. After many discussions, Jacob became a child of the collectives, moving every week or so among the four- or five-member households. The men encountered more opposition to taking Jacob to work with them than did the women, and for some—the construction worker, the bank teller, the kitchenworker at the hospital—it was impossible at that time.

I was by now a college professor, one of the grannies of the group. My research and action centered around women and work; I shared salary and tasks within the group. Mom and Dad, by now old, still rural and of modest means, still small-town Republican, came to visit once. (Dad walked in with two sleeping bags under his arm, looked around, cleared his throat, and said: "Ah, this is a nice 'pad' you all have here.") They took the politics, posters, and unfamiliar sexual orientation of some in stride. They were pleased but surprised at a healthy, expressive, and self-disciplined Jacob, but they couldn't go along with deprivatized possessive biological relationships. *That* was family.

Like many social anarchists, we were very disciplined and often overdid organization. (Once, when Dan was to create some kind of entertainment at a party, he got stoned instead with his buddy, and was criticized at the next meeting for failing to create spontaneous joy at 8:30.) So we learned as we went.

Cooperation has never meant the absence of conflict. Conflict is as inherent in human interaction as cooperation; it is impossible to strive for one without creating the other. Our group faced problems common to other cooperative endeavors, such as the need for value similarity (Rothschild and Whitt 1986), and, common to collectives in general, problems of family, sexual relations, and alliances (Talmon 1972; Barrett and McIntosh 1983). We did not face some problems endemic in large, industrial producer cooperatives, such as concentration of scientific and technical skill among a few (Rothschild and Whitt 1986).

All of us had notions of how industry and work might be organized. Then, in the mid-seventies, came word of the Mondragon producer cooperatives in the Basque Country of northern Spain. This system of 19,000 worker-owners in over a hundred firms embodies the structural principles of organization we had come to believe were most productive of good workplaces and community. They not only worked, they thrived. It was ten years before I could go to see for myself, and to explore the status of women in the Mondragon cooperatives and in Basque society. Now, after years of collaboration with Barton Hacker, my work centers on gender, technology, and cooperation, and I have recently returned from sabbatical in the Basque Country of northern Spain.

This chapter is in part a reflexive statement, illustrating some of my experiences and probably the gut-level "structure of sentiments" that Gouldner (1970) says we use to evaluate the power of a theory. We like explanations that resonate with those sentiments, and judge them to be more adequate than others. Thus our experiences inevitably color our viewpoint, and it is wise to share these with a reader.

We are only beginning to realize how most interpretations of social phenomena are colored by experiences shared largely by men. A forthcoming work by Fonow and Cook richly illustrates the constraints placed on the social creation and interpretation of events when these include no woman's perceptions. In Chapter 2–4, I add my own tales to the stories of technology and work.

I begin by telling about some research action projects on gender, technology, and work that take place from the late sixties to the present within different feminist theoretical perspectives: liberal, socialist, radical, and emergent feminist thought on the social construction of technology and eroticism. I think it is possible to learn from each. Sokoloff (1980), Eisenstein (1981), and Jaggar (1983) provide excellent general statements of feminist perspectives; I use a similar approach, applying it to these concrete cases of research and action. Part II of this book deals with alternative and oppositional constructions of gender, technology, and work, the potential of which may best be realized in cooperative structures. It focuses on the Mondragon experience and the centrality of gender for full, cooperative participation.

CHAPTER 2

Research, Action, and Theoretical Perspectives

This chapter describes three instances of feminist research and action linking gender, technology, and work. Each falls roughly within one of the three major paradigms of feminist theory found in the United States at the moment—liberal, socialist, and radical. The fit between theory and action, and the interpretation of each, is specific to place, time, and people. Moreover, although these were instances of more and less collective efforts, they are being recounted by one person. The strengths and weaknesses I perceive in each perspective must be taken in that context. Further, I experienced them in a particular sequence, so that my years among working women, who were by comparison older, more conservative, and less privileged, preceded my years of action among largely college-age and -educated socialists. My years of radical feminist research followed both these experiences, and thus may incorporate historical and materialist components to a greater extent than usual. The fourth approach to research and action outlined in Chapters 3 and 4 can hardly claim status as well-developed theory. It builds on my earlier work, and on ethnography in engineering education. This line of thinking emerges from my analysis of the military origins of engineering education, and from what I see to be related debates on technology and eroticism. It combines what I take to be most helpful elements of dominant perspectives into a version of social anarchist feminism.

My experiences have shaped by approach to gender, technology, and cooperation in general, and to the study of the Mondragon cooperatives in particular. I offer, then, some of the content and context by which feminist discourse may best be judged (Ferguson 1984).

18

Liberal Feminism

The first story is told from a liberal feminist perspective, and concerns women's employment in the American Telephone and Telegraph (AT&T) corporation between 1969 and 1976 (Hacker 1979a). In the late sixties, AT&T accounted for the greatest number of discrimination complaints by women and minorities. These AT&T workers, with the help of the National Organization for Women (NOW) and other civil rights organizations, took legal action to enforce equal opportunity in employment—equality within the system. I worked in Texas for four years, then Iowa for three, and in my spare time was the national coordinator of NOW's AT&T task force. We obtained company data, analyzed it, and saw that women were employed at lower levels, especially minority women. We worked and fought for equal opportunity in hiring, promotion, pay, and benefits. We wanted to see an even distribution of women and minorities from top to bottom of the corporation. This is a liberal feminist framework. It argues that all individuals be treated fairly within the company as it is. We argued on the basis of logic, efficiency, existing law, productivity, reason, and simple fairness. The NOW AT&T task force, including many phone company workers, wrote newsletters, shared information and strategy with women workers across the country, met with union and nonunion men and women, and argued our case with management and then in the courts. After three years of fighting to get data (and realizing the power of a large corporation to gather, shape, and control information), we began to realize we needed a more radical approach to research methodology. An analysis of four organizations, described later, suggested that corporate resistance to critical research—delaying and dissembling, lying, distortion of data—increased with the sophistication and professional training of the managment component (Hacker 1980).

In 1972 the U.S. government ordered AT&T to produce an affirmative action plan, a legal document showing intent to move women and minorities up the occupational ladder within a three-year period. It was true; the company did plan to do so. We saw, however, that more women were going to be moved out than up. A closer examination revealed that the company planned to eliminate 36,000 jobs, primarily those of operator and lower-level clerical worker. Belatedly, we had discovered the process of technological displacement, and that it affects women differently, at different times, than it does men. This for me began a lifelong study of technology and gender. I suggest that studies of technology and gender stay closely related to issues of women and work, especially workers at the bottom of the heap and women in developing countries (ISIS 1984; Nash and Kelly 1983). This will help ensure that action and research stay grounded in gender issues relevant to all women.

At AT&T, most women worked in jobs that had been technically simplified enough to be automated. The company preferred to reduce the work force through attrition rather than layoffs. Sometimes government-sponsored research showed how to do this, by making jobs less pleasant, speeding things up, tightening control (Bureau of Labor Statistics 1973). We had argued, among other things, that a restructuring of the operator's job would also slow turnover rates. We had calculated the savings to be gained thereby. We had not realized that high turnover rates were necessary for automation without layoffs.

The very organization of the company seemed to set people against each other. High-level systems group decisions were translated into daily action by low-level supervisors, often women, always unaware of overall plans. Many of their instructions and demands appeared mindless or stupid to many workers, who described being treated like children or like parts of a machine. Operators spoke about new standards requiring faster work, and a machinelike, limited form of communication. (One might almost have thought the company planned even to automate verbal communication.) Some women complained they were not allowed to help a caller as much as in the past. They had been proud of that work. Others spoke of a mystifying index of performance, yielding negative ratings, sometimes for tasks they had not been assigned, on days they were not on that job. They said these negative ratings inhibited their bids for transfer or promotion. One woman opened the mail on the night shift. At the end of her shift she was shown a tally sheet of time wasted in yawning and scratching.

The phone company, according to one executive, was designed by geniuses to be run by idiots. Supervisors, themselves in impossible jobs, can take it out on underlings. As the character in Toni Morison's (1970) story says of black people, women also "took as our own the most dramatic, and the most obvious of our white masters' characteristics, which were, of course, their worst. . . . We believed authority was cruelty to inferiors" (p.140). Co-workers were not immune to this desire for control over someone, anyone. Office workers kept a craftswoman waiting 20 minutes on top of a pole in an Iowa snowstorm while they jollied up her male counterparts with the story.

PROBLEMS WITH A LIBERAL FEMINIST APPROACH

We learned that the men's jobs AT&T was most willing to open to women and minorities were those they planned to automate next. White male skilled craft jobs such as switchman were being simplified, degraded, and given to minority males (Braverman 1974). Repair work was simplified, called "idiot maintenance," and given to women. Minority males held semiskilled jobs such as framework, line-assigning, or installing, which were being transformed by computer to sophisticated clerical work, and filled by white women at about half the pay. Minority women found easier access to some advanced-level clerical work, but work already in process of simplification. Most minority women had already routine jobs, as operators and entry-level clericals, soon to be replaced by machine. As these jobs disappeared, so did those of their female supervisors. In studies of other industries, with some exceptions, we found similar patterns: jobs undergoing technological change were held first by white males, then by minority males, white women, minority women, and then machines. So we found ourselves in the position of arguing that women and minorities be hired exactly where the company wanted them—in jobs next to be automated. A phone worker told me, "A white man can't get a job at Bell these days," and blamed the process on affirmative action.

The lawsuit against AT&T ended in a settlement that repaid millions of dollars in back pay to thousands of female and minority workers. There was substantial media coverage from coast to coast. It was the largest civil rights settlement to date. It did open nontraditional crafts to more women and minorities. It did help convince the union to take stronger stands on civil rights issues and on automation. But we had not changed the structure of the corporation, which led to such peculiar and unfortunate authority relations, nor had we affected the process of decision-making about technological change, technological displacement of workers, or the pitting of man against woman, Anglo against black and Hispanic, each against all.

We continued for a while in the liberal framework. We explained to management what was happening. Many middle-level and some upper-level managers in the various Bell companies were as surprised as we were. They seemed truly chagrined that the percentage of women employed anywhere in the company was decreasing with every step toward moving women and minorities up. They vaguely believed that new techology created new jobs. They had not noticed that jobs eliminated were generally held by women and minorities, and that the jobs created were filled by white men with computer skills, by and large. But that was progress.

At the highest levels of the corporation, executives were neither surprised nor sorry. We learned that the corporation had articulated plans some 15 years earlier to replace male craft workers with females, then with machines. Women's labor was cheaper, and women did not fight back as much as men when the work was eliminated. The executives had used affirmative action to ease the company's struggle with unions to replace male with female craft workers. They were not irritated that feminists bothered about the technological core of the company, rather than sticking to affirmative action for equal opportunity, where we belonged.

This is where most of us are, I believe—holding a liberal feminist position and arguing for equality within the system. After several years in this action, and in the Iowa collectives, some of us came to think we should also be somewhere else.

Marxist and Socialist Feminism

This was a time of multiple memberships, such that many activists were members of feminist, liberal, and radical left groups, peace or antimilitary and civil rights groups. We learned a lot from each other, and people were changing. For example, one task force in the Des Moines chapter of NOW began with a few complaints that Boy Scouts got more money than Girl Scouts. It finished with a large number of people, and an impressive critique of sexism, racism, capitalism, and voluntarism in general, and United Way in particular (Noun 1974; NOW 1974). Corporations had strong-armed clerical workers earning less than poverty wages to "give their fair share" to largely middle-class or male organizations served by the agency. This task force held public hearings and debates, met with unions, talked at churches. They located the source of social problems squarely within a society that would leave its most important tasks to be funded by bake sales and unpaid labor. The group wrote and performed a home-built musical to that effect, and performed it on public television.

Those of us active in NOW and the anarchist collectives described in Chapter 1 applied this new view of society to the contradictions faced by workers at AT&T. We learned more was at stake than simply cheaper labor. The company's phone rates were in part based on the amount of capital tied up in equipment. The more invested in machinery, the higher the rates could be. Corporation and state cooperated in depreciation regulations, setting the value of outmoded technology where AT&T would benefit. Further, military needs in telecommunications, such as radar, microwave, digital transmission, fiber optics, and satellite configurations, often distorted a technology shaped for civilian use (Shepherd

1971; Smith 1985). We learned how much of the social organization of AT&T and other corporations, from job descriptions and tests for acceptable personalities to management styles and the structure of research laboratories, was modeled on military processes (Noble 1977). But, most important at the time, we now saw AT&T as a giant corporation within a capitalist system, and learned how workers, and especially women, paid for corporate profit and bore the burden of technological change. Corporations, we argued, created technology in their own interest, and its form affected the everyday lives of all of us. Education about inequality would not suffice. Women's subordination was simply profitable, as was a divided labor force that could be manipulated easily.

Arguing a Marxist framework is difficult in the United States, where knowledge of economic systems is limited. "Socialist" and "Marxist" are equated vaguely with the Soviet Union and with lack of individual freedom. Movements for equality that "go too far" are labeled socialist or communist. This is often enough to turn people off, as it did many of the women with whom we worked. But some of the message seemed so clear. To increase profits, capitalists must decrease labor costs, among other things. AT&T invested in technologies that simplified and cheapened work, or replaced workers altogether. And one day, workers would not be able to buy back what they produced, leading to a crisis in the system. Then we write off one more generation of workers with "obsolete" skills, and many workers blame themselves for lack of jobs. The closer the language of theory to the stuff of everyday life of women, the better we could cooperate in joint action.

We talked with each other, wrote newsletters and pamphlets from a socialist perspective, argued with union leadership for women's rights and a stronger automation clause in the contract. This would be a first step toward worker ownership and control of the means of production. The approach, however, pointed out a soft spot in Marxist theory in that workers had very different experiences based on gender.

We argued that technological change in AT&T affected

women and minorities disproportionately, and thus, under civil rights legislation, should therefore cease until that was no longer the case. Nice idea, but even our own lawyers wouldn't touch it.

Media coverage of this new perspective—gender-equal worker control or participation in decisions on new technology—was less than helpful, for many reasons. Reporters welcomed the sudden AT&T settlement as a great step forward for women. But new socialist feminist stories, about the use of women and minorities as a "reserve labor army" to ease the path of automation were, according to one editor,"too complicated." Perhaps so. We might have become better storytellers. But his newspaper, along with many others, was in the process of its own technological revolution, eliminating skilled white male, typesetters in favor of computer-related clerical work.

We worked with women's groups, socialist groups, and unions, aiming to change the very economic foundations of society. Many workers, however, believed that their best interests were served by those very foundations, compared to any other alternative. And by and large, at that time, socialists and unions were as masculinist as was business. But we were beginning to recognize that somebody owned technology, and it didn't design itself.

PROBLEMS WITH A SOCIALIST FEMINIST PERSPECTIVE

In the AT&T action, there were the usual problems facing female workers. One very effective telephone worker stopped holding women's meeting when her husband—also a telephone worker—complained she no longer had time to take care of him and the kids, and *that* was family. Another women stopped her feminist activities when she married, to begin again after divorce. A group of union women worked long and hard to get feminist issues on the meeting agenda. At that point, their male co-workers voted to end the meeting in favor of a sports film.

Socialists at the time treated these and similar instances gingerly. All of these issues run the risk of dividing the working class—the primary unit of interest to Marxists and socialists. We encountered similar differences of interest, however, between working men and women among steel-workers, migrant workers, and craft and clerical workers.

At that time, there was little attention to women's special economic position with respect to the working-class man. At one socialist sociology meeting, we debated endlessly the question of which workers were working-class (and therefore legitimate co-revolutionaries). Could it be engineers? Well, maybe, maybe. Could it be college professors? Well, if they had been "declassed" (by losing their jobs), and on and on. Could it be telephone workers, operators? No. These were white-collar, middle-class women—even, according to one young academic, class enemies. In Marxist workshops, women's lives did not fit many of the models given, or the analysis. Sometimes we were told that those questions, the woman questions, must wait for another workshop.

While maintaining a Marxist analysis of capitalism, and its effects on the development of technology, we saw that the theory left something to be desired, especially where we needed to address gender and technology. Could it be our own misinterpretation or misapplication of theory? Perhaps, but if so it was a widely shared misdirection. In part our theories became better articulated with underlying assumptions, assumptions we barely noticed let alone analyzed, within the dominant perspective of liberal feminism. As our actions and discussions became better integrated with our theory, however, we began to lose touch with most working women. Our language had become far too abstract and off center from everyday concerns—problems with male co-workers, problems of family, sexuality, and authority.

Judith Stacey's (1983) recent work on patriarchy and the socialist revolution in China illuminates tensions between socialism and feminism. That revolution "democratized" the patriarchal family. Whereas before only the wealthy could maintain such a family, afterward any man could have one. The household remained the basic economic unit. Patrilocal and patrilineal forms were retained, resulting in what Stacey calls "patriarchal socialism." She argues that patriarchy may in fact be more compatible with socialism than with capitalism. The latter is such a vicious system that it destroys

26

traditional family while creating no new alternatives. This may explain the greater strength of feminism within capitalist than socialist countries. Socialism pays attention to human needs within a traditional family.

Marxist theory and often socialist practice do not apply a materialist analysis to patriarchy, or a feminist analysis to work and class, as Stacey wisely suggests we must do. Unless feminist goals are clearly articulated and equally emphasized, socialist revolution can lead to patriarchal socialism. Stacey's book is also important for the careful attention given the army in the democratization of patriarchy. This institution provides resources, solidarity, training, support, and experience helpful primarily to men.

Stacey's analysis was not available in the mid-seventies, but we had learned from experience in liberal and socialist practice that something more was needed on a theoretical level. There was more to the story than ignorance and lack of equality, more than profit and other dynamics of capitalism. This was particularly true for analysis of gender and technology, which we knew to be affected by forces other than capitalism. We began to read the work of radical feminists.

Radical Feminism

Radical feminism added a missing notion—that of gender subordination as a legitimate issue and a root problem in social organization. Gender subordination existed long before capitalism. It would take more than a new economic order to liberate gender. Gender stratification provided a model for all other forms of social hierarchy. Workers, the poor, people of color are ascribed womanly characteristics, particularly the inability to govern their own sexuality; they are nearly as close to nature as are women. This justified keeping them in their place. I was surprised later to find this model also works for men at the top, in ranking white males in prestigious occupations among themselves.

Radical feminism led to new critical perspectives on relationships, and integrated these with critiques of all major

27

social institutions. It linked the personal to the political in more powerful analyses than we had available before, demanding a deeper and more comprehensive interdisciplinary approach. Important for our study of gender and technology, this perspective drew attention to an older ideology, the gendered basis of bureaucratic organization, and domination over the natural, feminine world. Elsewhere in the literature, we tried to read between the lines of philosophers, historians of technology, social scientists, critical theorists, and others dealing with man's relationship to the natural world. Radical feminism provided explanations that better articulated the direct link between women's subordination as part of the domination of nature and the replacement of reason with technical rationality. Firestone (1970), Ortner (1972), Daly (1973), Kolodny (1975), and others cut through the masculinist bias in these critical analyses of domination. They suggested alternatives to the puzzling pessimism when gender was by and large ignored, even if sexuality was not. Most important, radical feminism encouraged the notion of women as independent agents of social change.

In particular, radical feminism was an excellent perspective for those of us working with women in agriculture and agribusiness in the early to mid-seventies. Again, women and minorities (this time migrant chicanas and chicanos) and small farmers in the Midwest were vulnerable to technological displacement (Hacker 1977a).

Family farmers cannot afford today's expensive agricultural technology or compete in a game where the large corporations and the state make the rules. In the fields, in the canneries, and in poultry and meat packing plants, agribusiness corporations replaced white with Hispanic labor and male with female labor and then machines, in another drive to reduce labor costs and increase profits. Power relations based on race and sex again hindered organizing in the packing plants; gendered power divided male from female migrant worker and farmer. Again, we could offer research and information as needed, work for progressive legislation, do grunt work for farmer or migrant actions, talk to people in the community, and help with demonstrations and boycotts that aimed to bridge the divisions between common people.

With a feminist perspective, issues of sex and race took center stage with the rest, and it was pretty tough going.

Migrant women shared the problems of their community, worked side by side with men (or behind, as a man operated farm machinery). In addition, chicanas were primary caregivers for their children, shouldered most responsibility for home and family, and faced community criticism for the condition of migrant housing (Hacker 1977a). One chicano organizer saw no alternative way to protect his daughter's virginity and therefore his own honor, and placed the teenager in juvenile detention. Differences between migrant men and women were best handled by the migrant women themselves, and by two chicana activists health workers. Health issues, however, were important to the community in general, and particularly so to women. Migrant women faced pregnancy with no relief; maternal death rates were more than 100 percent higher in the migrant community than in the Anglo. The Boston Women's Health Book Collective sent a draft of their first Spanish translation of *Our Bodies, Ourselves* (1973, 1976).

Among the Anglo farmers, we learned how women lost control of their land through divorce. Widows were more easily persuaded to rent or sell to corporations; corporations, equipment dealers, and financial institutions were less cooperative with women. We learned how the Farm Bureau and various industry organizations funded "educational programs" for farm women, encouraging their volunteer activism against organized labor, migrants, consumer groups interested in health and ecology, and feminists. In conversation on these small Iowa farms, however, it was generally the women who showed more understanding and concern for the condition of migrant families, and more antagonism for the operations of the corporations (in this case, contracting the farmers to grow tomatoes for catsup production). Big business, "bigger everything," as one farm woman put it, was destroying a way of life. Farmers puzzled over solutions, but women particularly seemed interested in information on alternatives.

Farmers worried about the chemicals they dumped on the land, but "progress" and the "need to feed the world"

29

demanded their use. No, they didn't know exactly what was in the chemicals. That knowledge belonged to the corporation and its scientists. Migrant health workers also collided with this private property of knowledge, unable to deal quickly and effectively with the health problems of migrant workers who came in contact with agrichemicals. This knowledge, generated in part by public-funded university research, belonged to the corporation, and legal battles to obtain it were slow and cumbersome.

Elsewhere I describe the wide range of methods necessary to overcome obstacles mentioned before—corporate lying, dissembling, and more sophisticated means of resistance to critical reseach (Hacker 1980). We used traditional analyses of existing data sets, content analysis, interviewing, ethnography, and less orthodox means to obtain public but hidden data; we once took a midnight motorcycle ride for a tour of a packing plant's night shift, when official records of Hispanic employees needed to be corrected by observation. We found that the best counter to corporate resistance was cooperative work with existing action-oriented community groups. Their information tended to be more accurate, and better organized to answer our inquiries, than more easily accessible official records. We combined morphological analyses of the structure of organizations and institutions with enthnography and participant observation.

During one summer, for example, I attended community college courses in crops, soils, petrochemicals, fertilizers, and marketing. In addition to more familiar political and economic ideologies, I noted, in many forms, an ideology of gender. These courses were driven by a patriarchal ideology. Classes were offered to young farm boys from lower- and middle-income families, whose chance to farm had already been forgone. I was the only female. In these agribusiness classes, the sturdy farm woman was often posed as the good women against the know-nothing, troublemaking urban woman who "didn't know beans from apple butter," needed a male expert in the supermarket to tell one cut of meat from another, and worried all the way from New Jersey about Iowa agrichemicals in the water supply. Contradiction between this ideology and behavior was obvious. While glorifying the

30

family-oriented farm woman, it was agribusiness itself that hastened the demise of the farm family, transforming farm woman into urban housewife or clerical or production worker.

The underlying emphasis on gender and sexuality in radical feminism shed more light on the ideology of agribusiness. Control—over nature, women, workers in general—was a dominant theme in most classes, especially marketing. Women were trivialized as sexy, dumb, or fit for routine work, certainly not for decision-making. Male-dominated occupations and industries were given higher or lower status by referring to them in masculine or feminine terms. Beef was manly; poultry was not. Horticulturalists were "long-haired flower sellers" (Hacker 1977a).

Lectures revealed a passionate concern for control over the reproductive processes of plants and animals. Gruesome stories of trial and error were told with relish (Hacker 1985). A whiz-bang technology lured some of the young farm boys in this class, but clearly turned others off. Spitballs and desk-etching picked up as the quarter progressed. But if you can't farm, your only alternatives seem to be jobs in marketing, sales, and manufacture. Once again, we noticed but did not analyze the role of the military—in research and development of pesticides and herbicides, in the petroleum industry, and as a major consumer of food and fiber products.

Repeatedly, in these research action projects, in telecommunications, newspaper, agribusiness, and other industries, managers with an engineering or technical background explained things, took actions, made decisions that often seemed heartless or at best bizarre. Sometimes it was a matter of a very different discourse. I asked one about technological change, jobs and people. He was truly puzzled; the data were not available to answer the question. He could not tell me about jobs and people, but about dollars and time. Not only did profit or control dominate decision-making, but sex and women provided a context for the rest of what was passed off as rational economic or technical analysis.

At engineering conventions, women in bunny suits staffed booths, advertised wares, had parts of their bodies measured in public spectacle by men pushing conversions to the metric system. A college fair boasted an agricultural engineering display with a leather-miniskirted mannequin, a sign on her rump stating "AG ENGINEERING—For a BROAD Education." Speeches at professional meetings began with an obligatory sexist joke. (The one I've heard most often turns around young college men sowing their wild oats and praying for a crop failure. Although this research took place more than ten years ago, I heard the same joke recently on my own campus, at a luncheon speech by the former state chancellor of higher education.) An issue of the *Iowa Engineer* devoted to professional ethics contained a sexist joke page (including the one about the coed given the question on which organ of the body can increase to many times its natural size, blushing, and being told she had a dirty mind for not thinking of the iris of the eye). The "E-girl" of the month posed on top of a filing cabinet.

I toured a printing plant where *Ms.* magazine was produced. The R&D manager told those of us who asked about the absence of *Ms.* on the display rack that they considered the magazine their "porno" department. Later he showed us the only place the company hired "girls"—the middle-aged women doing hand bindery work. Why? Men wouldn't sit still for that kind of boring work. This notion that ladies don't move was repeated in plant after plant. A metals plant manager told us men need to get up and move around; the jobs requiring sitting at repetitive tasks were for women. The poultry plant manager remarked similarly that men are more suited for beef rather than poultry processing, because you get to move around much more. He ventured to comment that "people" won't take poultry work anymore— only women and migrants would (see Cockburn 1985, on gendered physical movement at the workplace).

Sexist jokes, comments, and ideology among the technically trained managers differed perhaps only in degree from those of our colleagues in social science or humanities. But remarks of those who define work and jobs, and decide then who does what, seemed by comparison obsessed with sexuality and with women's place. These issues brought us in closer communication with other working women, who understood well how such an ideology set them against each other and fixed their place at work.

I wanted to understand how a patriarchal worldview was structured and passed on to the next generation of those who would organize work and technology. I was curious about the role of gender as well as sexuality, and how that affected the technology, the organization of work, and women's place within it.

PROBLEMS WITH A RADICAL FEMINIST PERSPECTIVE

A radical feminist perspective articulates the historical and contemporary function of such an ideology. But when one's first experience is with the writing of radical feminists, there may be a tendency to romanticize the womanly (nature) and to villainize the manly (engineering). Thus would we miss our mark. Deniz Kandiyoti (1984) points out that the primary purpose of patriarchy is not to control women, but to control other men. The older, more powerful men of a society subordinate and undermine the other men, who effectively limit the sphere of women. The opportunity for these men to retain power in turn over women may be an essential element in their acquiescence to their own subordination by other men.

Radical feminism takes us beyond the divided labor force and the reserve army of women controlled for profit, to the bases of gender hierarchy. It encourages a radical challenge to the structure and even the existence of the patriarchal family (Barrett and McIntosh 1982). It takes us into the realm of control over nature and our physical selves, our own mind-activated body, as Mumford put it. It warns us that the construction of gender, science, and technology are intertwined (Griffin 1978; Merchant 1980; Starhawk 1982; Keller 1985; Haraway 1985; Harding 1986). This perspective could suggest that it is in our best interest to learn how men are persuaded to give up autonomy, come to value a narrow, technical rationality over reason, and to accept as normal and right the contemporary forms of relationships, sexuality, eroticism, technology, work. At its best, it could incorporate the analysis of material and historical conditions affecting both men and women. Finally, it would not rest so heavily on a "bias" theory of antiwomen ideology alone, but could explore the system of institutional arrangements through which the dominant encourages us to take part in the gendering process (de Lauretis 1987). This participation perpetuates gender subordination even in the absence of prejudice and hostility.

Radical feminism could better explain ways in which we ourselves, women as well as men, come to support patriarchal institutions by taking part in them in our everyday lives.

I wanted to pursue these questions, such as social hierarchy in engineering. Who in their right mind would give up so much for so little privilege over others, and why? I wanted also to learn more about engineering from the inside out. I came to know it was not as much about ferris wheels and trolleys as it was about computers, petrochemicals, and missiles, to see that there was quite a distance between the backyard mechanic who designed and built and repaired and the scientifically educated engineer. I wanted to test some of the notions in radical feminist theory, and to learn what and why technologists felt and believed as they did.

CHAPTER 3

Discipline and Pleasure in Engineering

By the late seventies, research and action had come some distance from the struggle for women's equality in AT&T or food production, and now approached the source of that inequality itself. We explored systems of exploitation that made sexism and racism profitable. We looked more closely at the world of the technologist, particularly at the field of engineering and ideologies of control and dominance—over each other, over workers, minorities, women, the body, the natural world. These ideologies made inequality comfortable (Weber 1968). But what made the organization of technology as it is today appealing? Why *are* there so many men in engineering?

Elsewhere, I have described what I saw and heard in two years of researching engineers and their culture at MIT (Hacker 1981a). Professors' jokes in a class on telephony again trivialized workers, blacks, and women and the feminine, suggested female students would trade sexual attention for answers to problems they couldn't solve, and poked uneasy fun at the body itself through scatological humor. Jokes elevated technical expertise and opposed it to natural body functions such as smell and excretion.

Some fields of engineering—notably electrical and computer science—had more prestige than others. Their activities and skills were clean, hard, and fast. Civil engineering, in contrast, was much too involved in the natural and social world, too messy and encumbered by political and social obstacles for such status. The social sciences, with the occasional exception of economics, were described in terms similar to those used for women—soft, fuzzy, "noise," unpredictable, unscientific. Status accrued to the masculine world of speed, sophistication, and abstraction rather than the feminine world of nature and people. Thus, even among men at the top, gender stratification separated the men from the boys, as one student admiringly described the toughest courses. How did things get this way? How can we make sense of all this?

Feminist anthropology, history, and archaeology help us understand the transformation to patriarchal societies in the past; literature, psychology, and sociology can illuminate these processes and those that perpetuate a patriarchal ideology in one man's life today.

I interviewed a random sample, which turned out to be all men, of the engineering faculty. I contrasted these with a random sample of men, then, on the humanities faculty. The conversations suggest that childhood experiences of both left few fond recollections of intimacy with friends or family. Perhaps a masculine trait in general, this was especially true in engineering. "I didn't have personal feelings as a child," said one. Most had experienced sex-segregated childhoods. Aside from family, they had little contact with females. They therefore understandably reported being "puzzled" or "mystified" or "frightened" by girls, with whom they had little interaction. Ben Snyder's (1971) *Hidden Curriculum* sensitively documents the continuing and painful lessons in masculinity learned at the institute.

The engineering faculty, in contrast to men in the humanities, recalled fewer sensual pleasures in childhood, and placed more value on hierarchy in the world of work ("Science can only be done by a highly trained elite."). As for rotating or sharing tasks, some thought working more closely with craftsmen might improve engineering; none saw any benefit in learning about secretarial or clerical work (Hacker 1983d).

Engineers were considered the most appropriate men for management, according to one, "because they can treat people like elements in a system," a virtual echo of the telephone operators' perceptions of years before. Engineering was attractive to this professor because of its elegant simplicity and its mathematical structure; it was clean, hard,

36

and predictable. For another, it was very much the opposite of his hysterical mother.

The powerful, gendered metaphors we employ, Kolodny (1975) wrote, may shape our thinking about the social and the natural world. As long as we gender the natural world feminine, we will treat nature as we do women. Often this means we talk about the natural world with reverence and exhilaration, perhaps recalling experiences of pleasure and danger. But it may also mean that we treat nature in everyday life with indifference and exploitation, even a gleeful violation, "just to see what will happen."

How do we come to so separate ourselves from the natural world? When asked why we tend to gender the natural world as feminine, engineering and humanities faculty members alike called forth images of reproduction. In engineering: "the whole cycle of having periods and all that"; "childbearing"; "the earth gives plants as a women gives children"; "nature is where everything comes from, including children" (Hacker 1981a). Men in the humanities expressed this ancient theme as well, but also another, more common in non-Western cultures—that of women and nature as dangerous and unpredictable (hurricanes, stormy seas, withholding food through the vicissitudes of climate, for example). Later, in a seminar with engineers in industry, I discussed these puzzling remarks on danger. I had expected as much from engineers, not from men in the humanities. One chuckled and said they didn't have to worry about either. Engineers had both nature and women under control.

I had followed a line of radical feminist research and theory, from classroom jokes about technical elitism, the body, and inferior groups of people to interviews with technologists linking childhood pleasures with adult pursuits such as organizing work. Discussion offered reproduction as the link between women and nature; some thought both bore watching. Radical feminism worked fairly well as a theoretical framework; it seemed to explain much of what was going on in the organization of gender and technology. But it seemed to work best observing women and nature as the victim, and men as a dominant group whose members were very much alike.

But all engineers were not alike, any more than all men or all women were alike. Some seemed more driven than others, some more sensitive to ways gender entered their work. I wanted to know more about how it felt to be an engineer, or at least how it felt to be trained in this field. In the late seventies, then, I took a job at a western land-grant university with a large school of engineering. In my spare time, to explore the crosscurrents of the field, I enrolled as an engineering student.

The Engineering Classroom

Part of the appeal of engineering lies with extrinsic rewards. Especially in the United States, engineering is relatively well-paid work, perceived as the most likely route for the young working-class boy moving into the professional class. But the practice of crafting and engineering also yields intrinsic pleasures. Eugene Ferguson (1977) addresses historians of technology, and warns us all that we ignore this "exhilaration" factor at our peril. Engineers are enthusiasts rather than objective observers, and often express elation, excitement, and curiosity in their work. That is the topic of this chapter.

We may study gender and engineering in many ways. Some seek to encourage women into the field. Others focus feminist analysis on the products, say, of reproductive technologies, or labor process in the health industry (Glazer 1984), clerical work (Bose et al. 1987), or the transfer of technology to Third World countries. Women in development scholars (ISIS 1984; Ehrenreich and Fuentes 1981; D'Onofrio and Pfafflin 1982; Ward 1984; Grossman 1980; Nash and Kelly 1983) study the relationship of gender stratification, technology, and change to the international division of labor. Scholars in the history of science and technology draw our attention to the influence of patriarchal institutions on the organization of scientific and technical knowledge (Chapter 2). Later, I explore the historical and material origins and developments of a gendered engineering education in patriarchal military institutions.

At this point, however, I wanted to understand what I saw as a masculine eroticization of engineering. I had railed enough from the "outside" and felt a contradiction, a lack of balance in my approach to engineering as the core occupation in the study of technology. I also thought I might like it, and wanted to find out what it had going for it. Technology had been a great source of pleasure in my childhood.

What drew so many of us to engineering and the crafts? A constructionist perspective is helpful in understanding how and why we all take part in maintaining networks or microstructures of power in everyday life (Berg 1987). Ethnography lets you walk in the steps of another, experiencing the forces at play in the structure of institutions and situations. And so, to understand the experience of contemporary engineering students, during the early 1980s I became an engineering student in my spare time, and kept notes.

I had never lived on the West Coast, but understood its schools of engineering were larger, more hierarchical, with less interaction among levels—professor, Ph.D. student, research assistant, technician, craftsman—than at MIT; no one thought of clerical workers as part of the team (Hacker 1985). A young MIT dean trained at Berkeley recalled being warned against hanging out with the machinists or inviting them to his seminars. But one cannot compare a small elite institution such as MIT, which encouraged such mingling and hands-on experience, with a large land-grant college, bureaucratically organized and less well funded for hands-on lab experience, and pretend to have discovered regional differences. The two types of institutions yield a different "product"—one, the elite researcher, director of scientific and technological projects, and industrial executive; the other, the routine engineer, the engineer now in sales, or the administrative bureaucrat. Money and prestige, contacts and contracts, make a difference for the student, and for the institutions (Piercy 1985). Few instructors or classmates at the land-grant college school of engineering knew I was a professor on the other side of campus; most thought of me as a middle-aged returning woman student.

More than one social science colleague remained certain, despite my protestations, that I was really changing careers for higher pay.

Even at Oregon State Unversity I felt the influence of economic background, the power to buy what you or others think you need or desire. I signed up to take courses, one at a time, in mechanical engineering orientation, the calculus sequence, and statics. Actually, I looked forward to it. Always good in math and science, as Maccoby (1963) predicts of tomboys, I thought it would be a kick to get back into it. But we not only had to buy books, we had to buy calculators, too. From habit, I bought the cheapest of those approved for the course. The first day at "lab"—nothing more physical than chalk and a blackboard, offering an opportunity to ask the instructor an individual question if you stood in line—students glanced about, comparing their equipment with that of others. I did the same. My calculator was smaller and performed fewer functions. I was embarrassed. What to make of this? One could, I suppose, become Freudian, but more easily if one were male. Analyses such as *Learning to Labour* (Willis 1977) or *The Hidden Injuries of Class* (Cobb and Sennett 1973) capture better what I felt. Reflected in the eyes of others, I imagined: not smart enough to know what to buy; probably not able to, handicapped, a "loser" in the technical game from the start, for want of proper tools; probably not a serious student anyway. But growing up on modest means, we had always made do, and so I did.

At first, errors in the text drove me to distraction. I had expected the precision, accuracy, and reliability for which the field was known. I assumed a misprint or misplaced decimal was, in fact, correct. Later I loosened up. Nobody's perfect; jam it through until it works. The right answer to the question was the crucial thing, anyway.

I wondered how technical education at Oregon State University would differ from that in the Des Moines Community College, and from prestigious MIT, both of which were more closely linked to the world of work. I found, for one thing, the ideology was not so explicit as in the elite institution or the more proletarian community college. The following remarks are from my notes (Hacker 1985).

No sexist jokes. No racist jokes. No oddly intense concern with the natural world, the body, women, sexuality. In Mechanical Engineering Orientation, we began with no fuss. We learned about significant digits. We learned how to operate our hand calculators. We learned how to work problem sets. Many of them. Hours of work every day. There was something peculiarly relaxing about all this.

When I asked a calculus teaching assistant what to do when I had to work all day (I didn't say at what) and only the tired hours were left for working calculus problem sets, he sighed, and looked around for his next student. "Yes, you really must save your best hours for this. Mornings are best." Another time I turned in a problem set, only to have my grade reduced by 10 percent because I didn't staple the pages together.

My statics study group told me kindly, but in no uncertain terms, about some of the rules. This was a team effort. No one made it through on their own. For those better placed than us, this meant learning which fraternity had the answers to the problem sets, which plan to use at the next exam (phalanx, for example, putting the smartest down front with the next two staggered behind, and so on). Our group could only distribute the problems among us. I complained I wouldn't learn as much as if I did all the problems on my own. They patiently explained that nobody has that much time. They were right. Time was the important element. Problems consumed most of it. Getting them done meant going out perhaps once a week. "The best student really wants to be in the lab 24 hours a day," said one.

Women students learned not to stop studying whenever their boyfriends were ready to stop. Students had to be very disciplined, especially with their pleasures. We worked toward the tests, not for understanding.

I finished one calculus exam and followed a young woman out the door. She threw up in the bushes. I walked her across the street. "It happens all the time," she explained, "happens to a lot of the students, [but] you get used to it." Another said "I may have been superior, but I hope I'm never that miserable again." One young man, quiet, Anglo, engaging, brilliant in these things (I thought), loved mathematics as he did life itself. But he could not pass calculus tests under the pressure of time. He dropped out, and changed fields.

I asked one statics professor why we couldn't have two hours instead of one for the exam. His response highlights an important function of timed tests: "If we gave the students more time, anyone could do it. The secretaries could even pass it." An instructor in civil engineering voiced his own resentment: "90 percent of you would make good engineers, but only 40 to 50 percent will graduate."

What ameliorates this tension? The intrinsic pleasure of math and science courses. Also firm, clear parameters, inelastic time, problems to solve with clear and singular answers, timed tests. There was, as the professors at the institute had explained, something clean, hard, simple, and elegant about all this. I longed for the quiet hours in the evening, watching the secant, which never came to a single point, sweep toward the magically intangible tangent. Or seeing a curve take shape in the mind's eye. I came to a somewhat better understanding of the engineering faculty I had interviewed earlier. And remembered that some of the best said they had avoided tests and homework as much as possible (see also Levy 1985).

I also noticed that people began to treat me differently. There were fewer pressures on my free time, less demand for extra work by students, colleagues, the university, and community groups and organizations. Before, even being sick had not let you off the hook; people certainly hoped you could get better in time to pitch in. But now I found all I had to say was "I've got calculus to do" or "I'm not finished with my problem sets." There seemed an immediate acknowledgment that nothing else could be that important.

Further, to my surprise and dismay, I found I was less willing to listen to students. In my office, I tapped my fingers, grew restless, and looked at my watch when conversation veered toward the personal; I wished they would take themselves to the counseling center, where someone specialized in that sort of thing. I had important work to do; I had to work my problem sets.

I talked about this in class with my sociology students. One, a doctoral candidate in student services, pointed out that the increasing division of labor, the separation of abstract mental work from all else, affected the role of professor, too. His field has originally, of course, comprised tasks expected of the professor before students' personal needs were "differentiated out" into another, lower-status profession (McGuire 1984). Other students were concerned as to whether the process was "reversible." So was I. I said I thought it was, but it probably left its mark. And I stopped taking engineering courses.

Most students suffer through all this without considering how else it might be done. Some students enjoy it. And the pressure is so constant, any let up feels extremely pleasurable, it is fun, feels good, exciting, to be so quick, so skilled in esoteric ways, to "get a good grade," to be part of an elite. Cockerham (1973, 1977, 1978) has studied this appeal, which seduces largely working-class men into the Green Berets or the paratroops in similar ways. And after all, it seems simply efficient that the smartest people should get the best jobs and be paid more. It is a rare engineering student who questions the operational definition of "smart." I did not meet one, even among those who flunked out. And I found myself, one sunny day, with a fresh "A" exam under my elbow, smiling at everyone I met.

In the advanced divisions of the science and engineering colleges, and among some faculty, of course, people questioned the organization of technical education, the projects unfunded, the importance of your "attitude" for your professional and intellectual life or death. People were also concerned about such issues as ecology and equality, though such soft concerns could discredit one's identity as a serious professional. At the lower levels where I studied, students seemed at once both more naive and more cynical. For example, the one day we spent on "Ethics in the Profession" was devoted primarily to questions on how to get around the codes. As before, many students seemed alienated, in both senses of that term, and knew it. How did we handle this?

As students, in agribusiness, then engineering, we adjusted to alienation in several ways—tuning out, segmenting classroom experience from our own personally defined lives; identifying with the math or the machine when personal relations became too difficult and complex; laughing on cue; being seduced by membership in a private club; finding interesting and gratifying social relations in work or study groups; learning the rules of the game and playing it well; using the prestige of technical expertise to curtail demands on energy and time from such publicly unrewarded distractions as family and community.

We also resisted, in sometimes fragile form: spitballs and desk etching; questioning and talking back; sharing with others how we felt; reading history; getting sick; dropping out; or, as in this book, taking notes and writing about it (Hacker 1985).

Gender, Skill, and Pleasure

I had also glimpsed something of the exhilaration and sensuality I had associated with technology as a child. It was different, more abstract. In the old days, the days of backyard mechanics, technology was tangible, accessible, visible. You could see, feel, smell, taste, and hear it. And you could move with it. Technology had indeed still been gendered; my sister and I, after all, only watched and played. We did not build.[1] Now the skills were different—abstract and intellectual, separated from crafting and building, more remote from social interaction, and still wonder-working.

Relying on movies and novels a century out of date, I had thought an engineer designed, built, maintained, and repaired when necessary. So did many of my classmates. It is surprising how many do not know exactly what an engineer does today. The tools, for example, require few bodily movements other than the finger on the key. When it became clear our primary tools were to be computers, calculators, or perhaps pencils, some left for the hands-on

44

work of the community-college-trained technician, who gets "to do the *fun* stuff," according to a utility engineer.

Real engineering was structured to draw and keep students disciplined with a special set of skills, yielding the camaraderie and elitism of in-jokes, private language, and delight in abstraction, complexities, and the elegance of the simple solution. Design gives you a chance to shine, but usually within a highly articulated framework of "how to." As Weizenbaum (1976) notes, the programmer can create worlds over which he or she has near total control.

The definition of skill is intricately involved with definitions of gender. Cynthia Cockburn (1983, 1985) has described the way in which masculinity is woven into many craft jobs, such as typesetting. The rugged characteristics— getting dirty, heavy lifting, using large tools and muscle—are traditional components of working-class masculinity. Rites of initiation and apprenticeship ensure and strengthen this masculinity. When typesetting became a computer job, some men had difficulty dealing with work they had defined, perhaps in defense of class, as feminine. The new work was soft, clean, and required mental skills alone. Now masculinity had to be redefined, its source abstract knowledge. At least this knowledge kept them superior to the mechanic, the semiskilled, the unskilled, and especially to women. So it was an important collective effort to keep these people out of the occupation, too. Calculus, as we will see in Chapter 4, provides this function for engineering.

Eroticism, Technology, and Gender

Technology is a passionate project for many of us. Although Ferguson (1977) did not mean to limit exhilaration to eroticism, I believe it is important to explore relationships between technology and eroticism, an expression or design strongly motivated by sexual desire. I believe the two were more closely woven in many prepatriarchal societies (Hacker 1987d), as Mumford (1967–70, 1972) has suggested. Engineering, the apparent epitome of cool rationality, is shot through with passion and excitement. It is as though an intricately controlled erotic expression finds its most creative outlet today in the design of technology. The phallic imagery of missile systems and the reproductive metaphors surrounding creative destruction have escaped no one (Easlea 1983; Cohn 1987; Edwards forthcoming), but that is hardly all there is. Describing their feelings about technology, some men talk about God, glory, honor, and other noble sentiments. Much of their talk, however, is also sexy and gendered.

Samuel Florman (1976), wealthy contractor and spokesman for technologists, conveys the excitement of technology, the passionate relations between men and machine, by quoting from literature. Engineers, he says, have yet to express their own powerful feelings about technology.

From Frank's "Panama Canal slashing its way through the tropical jungle: Its gray sobriety is apart from the luxuriance of nature. Its willfulness is victor over a voluptuary world that will lift no vessels, that would bar all vessels"; from Kipling, on how the "feed-pump sobs and heaves"; Spender's airliner, "more beautiful and soft than any moth, with burring furred antennae . . . gently, broadly she falls"; McKenna's description of engineer meeting engine. "'Hello engine. I'm Jake Holman', he said under his breath. Jake Holman loved machinery in the way some other men love God, women and their country"; Longfellow's ship who "feels the thrill of life along her keel" as she "leaps into the Ocean's arms!" Platonov's engineer who enters "into the very essence of the abstruse, inanimate mechanisms . . . actually feeling the degree of intensity of an electrical current as if it were a secret passion of his own"; the pilot who "passed his fingers along a steel rib and felt the stream of life that flowed in it . . . the engine's gentle current, fraying its ice-cold rind into a velvety bloom." (Hacker 1985: 129, based on Florman 1976:124–139)

Whew! This is pretty steamy stuff. But what about real live women? Florman cites the engineer who says, "I'm in love, Chief." He hears from his boss, "So was I once, but I shut myself up for a week, and worked at an air machine. Grew so excited I forgot the girl. You try it" (Florman 1976:138). (See also Levy 1985 for an up-to-date expression of eroticism in the work of computer hackers.)

This peculiar masculine eroticizing of technology is limited to neither technologists nor conservatives. It shows itself across the political spectrum, as witness Woodie Guthrie's "Grand Coulee Dam." True, he wrote for the Bonneville Power Association, but he was not a man to adjust his creativity solely to the dollar. The problem lies not in eroticizing technology alone—I suggest that is unavoidable—but in the limited routines from which we draw.

Remarking on the obvious appeal of more accessible technology, Ferguson also sees complexity itself as sensual. This is true of the abstract skills of "high technology" as well (Kidder 1981; Levy 1985). But now more of the pleasure than before seems shaped by hierarchy, prestige, and power over others, rather than, as I recalled, doing a job and having fun. Pleasure was now more often about dominance and control. Dominance has been eroticized, notes Valverde (1987) in her study titled *Sex, Power and Pleasure*. This seems to me as true in engineering as in the world of sexuality in general.

Along with other things, we learned some of these rules in class. As students, we submitted to the routine, more than to the professors, though some enjoyed that scene as well. Largely, however, the discipline of daily life was impersonal. We did it to ourselves, and felt a sense of camaraderie in our mutual suffering. An occasional student beat the system, say, by cheating, but resistance was sporadic and largely individual.

Most students sought to dominate their fellows at a distance, largely in terms of grades and ranks. Degrees, grades, and information were crucial to this exercise, but so were other aspects of the ideology, such as the professors' classroom jokes described in Chapter 2. Dominance later must be exercised in a qualitatively different manner over the crafters and builders, about whom the new technologists seemed so uneasy (Noble 1984). In his deconstruction of computer science textbooks Sørensen (1984) shows how workers can be made to disappear as people. In the masculinized formulations of the field, in the gendered organization of knowledge, working-class people can become inanimate elements in a system (see also Edwards 1986b).

Learning engineering could have been more fun. In *To Engineer Is Human*, Petroski (1985) does not tackle the problems of networks of power in engineering or between engineering and the society in which it is set. His is not a critique of engineering, but it shows a loving touch with the field. It playfully likens the body and its functions to levers, cranes, balances, all the simple machines, showing how much we know, naturally, about engineering because we ourselves, our physical selves, learn to walk, to move, to lift babies, to turn, all in kinesthetic relationship with our environment. In Chapter 8, we will explore similar programs specifically for girls. My experience in engineering, however, came closer to Foucault's (1979:146) "Roman comedy of the classroom," a technology of power. Discipline for the sake of control, the expression of someone else's desire, rather than also self-expression.

In the experience of becoming an engineering student, I learned how it felt, day by day, sometimes minute by minute, to encounter a subtle control, largely self-imposed, that affects both mind and body. I learned many of the faculty were as turned off by the hidden curriculum as I, and felt the focus on math and grades impaired the student's ability to learn to do good engineering (Hacker 1983a). The discipline was intense—particularly over other pleasures, given that time was inelastic. One usually had to find pleasure in accepting a problem as given and following strict rules for its solution. I also felt the seductive power of special privileges, and of the delights and fascinations of the field. I saw how others reacted as well, as holding back their demands on my time and energy now that I was doing "important" work.

In engineering education and practice, much depends on supporting the hierarchical structure of the various bureaucracies so many engineers call home. Such patterns of dominance over underlings and submission to authority have their parallels in eroticism as well. It is possible that a society whose major forms of organization are hierarchical must capture and shape eroticism in similar authoritarian molds. Thus, both technology and eroticism shape each other and society, but also reflect dominant patterns of interaction within society as well.

The discipline of the classroom in a sense eroticized power

relations—glory and status in pain given or taken, or pleasure withheld; the postures of superiority or dominance and submission; a fetishism with special equipment and technique. I thought these linkages were more striking, more dramatic at MIT. Regardless, like the military, it was a game among boys and men. The very presence of women spoiled the sport.

What did that feel like from the inside? We were all an elite. Why? In part because we could discipline our pleasures, we could "take it," but for public consumption, it was because we could pass the tests. And so, we didn't have to do the work others, primarily women, had to do. What about the women students? Generally, we became "one of the guys."

From one coast to another, women engineering students have shared their relief upon finally being accepted by the men in engineering as one of the guys. Some voice their resentment, not quite sure of what, since it is surely a sign of upward mobility from being a girl. As Cockburn (1985) notes, however, being one of the guys means, for women especially, suppressing sexuality and with it a good part of the spontaneity needed for creativity in the field.

Some say that gender itself is dissolving, that now women can be masculine, men feminine. We can practice masculine patterns of both technology and eroticism. For example, we can study engineering; we can be sexually aggressive. In part, these activities can be pleasurable in and of themselves. Women's entry into the traditionally masculine is important, but it is only one aspect of degendering technology and eroticism. It strengthens the masculinization of both and includes but few women. Our participation in these traditionally masculine activities produces tremendous contradictions, for us and for the field.

During periods of rapid change, there are transformations in both technology and gender. Contradictions come to the fore—between traditional gender and equality, and within the concepts of masculine and feminine. At this time, despite women's participation in engineering or in a traditionally masculine eroticism, there is little change in the underlying material conditions that maintain men's superior power with respect to women.

Technology and Eroticism

We can learn from the parallels in debate over technology and eroticism, centered as they are on sensual and intellectual pleasures. I suggest that the current forms of both technology and eroticism emphasize relations of dominance, control, and submission. These tendencies originate deep in military institutions. Military institutions, even more than religious, must control erotic and technical activities in patriarchal society, locking both on an authoritarian dimension. I return to this theme in Chapter 4. For now, I would like to compare aspects of these two debates.

In the early 1980s, a legitimate concern for sexual violence and abuse of women and children led feminists to a sometimes one-dimensional picture of woman as victim and male sexuality as aggressive and dangerous. One strategy is to eliminate the stimulus for aggression some judged to be pornography.

Women workers in the sex industry, however, launched a surprising counterattack.[2] They argued that feminists went "over the heads of the workers," threatened their employment and dignity in work. This Marxist language compels attention. "Sex radicals" also use a feminist language, and members of this vociferous minority say they enjoy sexual games of power and domination, even violence. Who is to define sexuality for them, anyway, and wasn't feminism supposed to liberate sexuality for more freedom of choice? In response to concerns for children, they argued against the continuing repression of children's sexuality.

The practice behind these discussions is varied. Cultural feminists—so-called by the left to indicate lack of materialist analysis—object to pornography or themes of dominance or submission, but may tend toward the politics of the powerless, seeking protectors, defining only one range of alternatives as the whole of wholesome sexuality. Women workers in the sex industry, on the other hand, may show more solidarity with those who own and control the "means of production" than with other working-class women. Further, sex radical texts display prescriptions for the proper care and use of sadomasochistic toys and tools (see Samois 1982). As Ehrenreich et al. (1986) say, S&M demands equipment.

This volatile exchange produces very thoughtful analysis. Radical feminists search for historical connections between sexuality and fascism (Griffin 1981). Spinrad's (1972) *Iron Dream* spoofs this phenomenon and its trappings, in a science fiction satire on fascism and eroticism. (In this novel, the attention to uniform dress is matched perhaps only by the space given costume and uniforms in military museums around the world.)

New insights from progressive feminists promise to maintain gains made by women to define their own sexuality (Snitow et al. 1983; Valverde 1987; Ehrenreich et al. 1986). And in the field of semiotics, Teresa de Lauretis's *Alice Doesn't . . .* (1984) considers the way gender of the subject modifies interpretation of codes and messages in erotic discourse. In the field of computers, Sørensen (1984) does a similar unwrapping of gender and power in the deconstruction of systems analysis textbooks.

There is no single, negative term like *pornography* for a kind of technology that rouses prurient interest, demeans the powerless, eroticizes domination, or offends along a moral dimension. Some would say that describes all of modern technology. Some would say *pornography* describes all of modern sexuality. We could all think of technologies that fill this bill, such as the short hoe recently outlawed for migrant farm workers, nuclear weapons, tools of torture, and chemical technologies for the exciting and often eroticized domination and control of nature. Many do describe such technologies as pornographic.

Some, like the sex radicals, agree that such technologies are pornographic, but like it that way. Some have described to me the beauties of napalm, difficult to understand without "being there": "You really have to see it in action to appreciate it." Or the excitement of watching weeds "grow themselves to death" in the search for chemical defoliants; the challenge to implant the embryo of a calf into the womb of a rabbit for cheaper transportation to a Third World country; or the curiosity about whether or not a

51

bioengineered calf will be too large for live birthing.

Mumford's (1967–1970) megatechnics or Winner's (1977) authoritarian technics seem somewhat bland descriptions of the technologies described above, which so specifically eroticize domination, as in tools and training designed to inflict pain on a helpless prisoner, perhaps for the erotic gratification of the captor. Bart Hacker suggests coining another term, *pornotechnics*, for the prostitution of technology, paralleling the term *pornography* for the prostitution of art. (Hacker 1987d)

Similar problems would surround such a term, however. For example, some of us may find our favorite forms of technological excitement classified as politically incorrect—the rides we love to scare ourselves with at the carnival, the fast cars and motorcycles of our young (and not so young) adulthood, the risks we willingly share with others in outdoor adventure, the chemicals we wear and consume, designs made purely (we think) for the fun of it, or new waves of software developed on military funding.

Much of the definition of approved sexuality and technology has to do with power. Some would no doubt decide they knew what was best for the rest of us—that, say, certain classes of people couldn't handle a particular technology. It is not difficult to imagine who might be morally offended if the working class, women, or the enlisted soldier gained skills in certain "command" technologies (Noble 1984; Smith 1985).

Women and workers are "good" if they use the equipment of technology or eroticism in prescribed ways, but dangerous and "bad" if they take things into their own hands. Women and men are divided between and among themselves by a system of stratification based in part on current definitions of technical or erotic skill, both defined by men of the upper-middle and upper classes. Upstart individuals confront conservative and radical alike about the politically correct use of these skills.

With both technology and eroticism, sometimes we may merely delight in the exercise of technique or skill for its own sake, while remaining distant from deeper involvement in process or goals of the project (as Tom Lehrer [1987] suggests for Werner von Braun, Simmel [1984] claims for the flirt).

A deeper understanding of each concept—eroticism and technology—can inform the other. There are illuminating parallels. Feelings about each set of activities are shaped early in life and inscribed on the body through kinesthetic experience (Snitow et al. 1983; Gouldner 1976). These activities have been sharply gendered, and often presumed biologically based, but recent scholarship attends to the social construction of each (Collins and Pinch 1982; Ehrenreich et al. 1986) and sometimes of both together (Edwards forthcoming; Cohn 1987; Sørensen 1984; Hacker 1983a). Both technology and eroticism leave some people cold, but fire the imagination of many. Some prefer theirs tinged with domination or danger, others prefer theirs to emerge gently in relations of long-term commitment and democratic participation.

According to some, distorted technology and eroticism victimize women and nature, while others argue for the right to express playfulness, creativity, and individuality in ways they see fit. Still others see both as myths, diversions from the more significant issue—relations of power. A few argue for maintaining dialogue, keeping the debate open on the nature and meaning of each.

In my experience, working-class women are less likely than others to have the current "politically correct" line on either (democratic technics or an anticensorship stance), but are more likely to explore innovations in both (see Baumann 1987). Such an unacknowledged class difference may throw debate awry, as various groups compete for allegiance of the working women.

Elsewhere I have examined the debates over pornography and technology more closely for the light each sheds on the other (Hacker 1987d). Here I want merely to show the close connection between eroticism and technology, and suggest they flow from similar wellsprings of human sensual pleasure. Our pleasures have been shaped in part to maintain authority; together, we can reshape them to strengthen reciprocity.

Technology, Pleasure, and Cooperation

Technology and eroticism—that which is designed to arouse sexual desire—are conditioned by power relations in everyday life. In Ehrenreich et al.'s (1986) exploration of the sexual revolution, they note that "meaning," "mystery," and "romance," which many fear will disappear in today's more open sexual negotiations, are in fact euphemisms for *obfuscation*. Such terms hide the subordination of women and inhibit their sexual spontaneity. Professional jargon, a mysterified discourse, does the same for the student in engineering.

Silence and hypocrisy, Ehrenreich et al. say, leave us where we were. Those who deny a free lunch to a hungry child would also link sexuality to reproduction; those who suspect welfare mothers of loafing would replace family planning and sex education with chastity centers:

> Yet it is precisely this punitive mood that most challenges us to pick up the lost thread of sexual liberation. If the "real issues" are economic deprivation, the threat of nuclear holocaust, the destruction of the environment, and so forth down the grimly familiar list, then we should perhaps acknowledge that the issue of human pleasure is not, after all, so marginal or secondary. For the "real issues" only reflect our vast, collective separation from the body, from the earth and other life on it, and from the possibility of delight in ourselves and each other. We may have come to the point where we no longer have the luxury—and puritarism can be a perverse kind of luxury—of dividing what is "real" from what is only personal; what is public, from what is most deeply felt. We may finally be obliged, by the very threats we have created for ourselves, to rethink pleasure as a human goal and reclaim it as a human project. (Ehrenreich et al. 1986:207–208)

Those of us outside what we consider technology may not have the luxury of allowing its current definition to cheat us of the pleasure to be gained through technological skill.

Not only technology, but gender also is in a period of transformation. "Masculine" and "feminine" are concepts that order much of our perception and apprehension of the natural and social world. I have suggested ways in which this major orienting principle, gender, may capture erotic energy in the patriarchal structures of our lives. But notions of gender are changing (Haraway 1983; Stacey 1987), masculine blurring with feminine. The elimination of gender is a radical step, most threatening to person and society. It unravels traditional patterns of eroticism, for new, alternate, oppositional forms increasingly defined by women (Ehrenreich et al. 1986). We would do well, I believe, in our study of technological development, to stay closely in touch with changes in the notions of gender and eroticism. Technology and eroticism have a common base; it is possible to fuse them once again, this time in relationships of mutality.

Foucault (1978–1986) suggests that the discourse on sexuality is also about power and alliances, bodies and desire. I believe that the discourse on technology is, too. Inequality takes many forms; here I am concerned with inequality based on gender. Social patterns currently favor men over women, and the social construction of both technology and eroticism reflects primarily the desires of men.

These designs will at times reflect the hostility and suspicion this dominant group has for us, the subordinated group. Ann Kaplan (1983) describes the "male gaze" in the construction of pornography. Men see, view, paint photograph, write. That gaze may idealize women or watch us with hostility. Women as active agents, however, can create new forms of eroticism. Filmmakers, photographers, or authors could image both a male and female gaze, Kaplan says, that can lead to an unconscious delight in mutual gazing.

I think our task in both erotricism and technology is to discover what kind of life for children, what kinds of societies, are most likely to ground pleasure in such unconscious delight and mutuality.

Both technology and eroticism are defined predominantly by men and stratified by gender. But there are differences among men as well, as in those among the three technical classrooms in which I studied. At the most and least prestigious institutions, the Institute and the community college agribusiness program, educators presented a conservative ideology, often through humor, and explicated the value of technique. In the large middle-level land-grant university, students learned this lesson implicitly, primarily through the process of daily life in school. Hands-on or elite and abstract, all emphasized the superiority of men over women. The technical, craft, engineering, and management project is masculine. These are central dimensions of a patriarchal structure.

In my stint as engineering student, I had tried to see some ways in which patriarchal ideology and practice managed to control young men's passions and loyalties today. I had learned that, in part, these patriarchal habits are often developed in the minutiae of everyday life, and that most all of us supported them by taking part, going along. As for me and the working-class and middle-class students learning to engineer, for farm boys in agribusiness classes, everything we learned to value, the life-style we came to desire, the prestige, income and status over others, all were perceived possible only by passing the tests. This daily experience required control of sensuality, the emotions, passion, one's very physical rhythms. As Foucault (1979) would say, it is indeed inscribed on the body. A general form of domination, it includes observation, recording, calculation, a whole set of "regulations . . . relating to the army . . . for controlling or correcting the operations of the body." (Foucault 1979:136). Foucault traces the emergence of the modern disciplinary society through the seventeenth and eighteenth centuries, and, like Mumford, locates its source in a peculiar dream:

> Historians of ideas usually attribute the dream of a perfect society to the philosophers and jurists of the eighteenth century; but there was also a military dream of society; its fundamental reference was not to the state of nature, but to the meticulously subordinated cogs of a machine, not to the fundamental rights, but to indefinitely progressive forms of training, not to the general will but to automatic docility. (Foucault 1979:169)

I had by now developed a healthy curiosity about the origins and development of engineering education, and the role of discipline through mathematics and testing. The constructionist approach was indeed enlightening. But this perspective, or perhaps the way in which I understood or used it, lacked for my taste sufficient power of historical and materialist analysis. Who benefited, as time went along, in a myriad set of conflicting and contradictory ways? If we don't know that, how can we better understand today's organization of technology, today's way of doing engineering education, and the forces that perpetuate it, and where its fault lines are?

The history of engineering education reveals it to be embedded in military institutions, which, in large part, define masculinity, a definition that varies by class. As outlined in Chapter 1, military institutions emerged some 5,000 years ago, coeval with women's structured subordination in society. These institutions also molded ancient, medieval, and modern engineering. Contemporary scholarship emphasizes the effect of military institutions on job design, management, laboratories; on communications, transportation, and manufacturing technology; on the purpose and style of higher education (Noble 1977; Smith 1985); and on the notions of gender. These are the themes of Chapter 4. The content of masculinity fits with the requirements for leadership and followership in bureaucratic organizations—control of sensuality, emotions, passion, one's very physical rhythms. Without such control, Kandiyoti (1984) says patriarchy is impossible, and Mernissi (1987) says no one would join armies. (Which is not the same as to say we wouldn't fight.) Today, we observe the contradiction of women entering an ambivalent set of institutions designed originally to keep them out.

In Chapter 7, we return to the organization of engineering and technical education in cooperative society, and to questions about how both technology and eroticism might be degendered. For now, the next step is to study the history of men and institutions that shaped engineering education.

Notes

[1] Institutions of engineering first allowed women into classes, but not laboratories. And computer equipment is not randomly distributed over the neighborhood schools of this country, nor do students have equal access by gender within them (Useem and Kimball 1983).

[2] Descriptions drawn from field notes, 1982–83, Los Angeles. See Hacker et al. (1984).

CHAPTER 4

Military Institutions and Gender Inequality

Military institutions are the central patriarchal institutions of civilized societies, and depend on the subordination of women (B. Hacker 1977, 1981, 1987; B. Hacker and S. Hacker 1987). They interact with and strongly influence all other major social institutions. They, not war, are the problem. As in the 1950s, they often exert their most potent design on societies in peacetime. Their influence is obvious in the various aspects of this research—AT&T at the time the fifth largest defense contractor; defense also the largest customer of the poultry plant. Many changes in the manufacturing labor process that affect not only operatives and craft workers but engineers as well had their origins in the military (Hacker and Starnes 1983; Noble 1984).

Military institutions deeply affect our concepts of gender and technology. These institutions employ most of our technologists; in many instances they employ most prostitutes, in this country and others (Phongpaichit 1982; Weeks 1986). They provide models for the Boy Scouts and other organizations interested in discipline and shaping the sexuality of boys. Once so formed, the military uses masculinity in its creation of soldier or "warrior" (Cockerham 1977). Military settings framed the residual image of the good women—June Allyson forever left behind, forever waving goodbye to her man in uniform, being protected (Steihm 1983), waiting. This good woman, like the farm wife of agribusiness literature studied earlier, contrasts with the bad woman spy, prostitute, or unfaithful wife or lover. The actual women in uniform, and in combat, is generally invisible (Enloe 1983).

In particular, AT&T was heavily involved in NIKE air

58

and missile defense systems, and helped determine the form of satellite communication systems (Hacker 1979a). AT&T's military involvement is not a new venture. At the turn of the century their executives worked closely with the military, creating new job descriptions and other changes in the labor process, particularly through engineering education (Noble 1977). It was not enought to know the corporation was involved in defense, and that it profited from hierarchies of race, class, and gender. I wanted now to understand the history of these patterns and why they so often occurred together. There were tensions between capital and state, which show themselves now in conflict between capital's need for cheaper engineering labor and the profession's defense of its boundaries (Hacker and Starnes 1983). There is also cooperation between the two. One way capital and military state worked together to accomplish social hierarchy was through control of engineering and technical education. This became the focus of my historical investigation. And so, in the early 1980s, stimulated by the experiences of the engineering classroom, I began to study the history of engineering. The role of military institutions came not as surprise, but as recognition. The relationship between military institutions and women's role in society is seldom tackled directly (for exceptions, see B. Hacker 1981, 1987, 1988; Enloe 1983).

The feminist significance of military institutions is this: they emerged with civilized societies in the fourth millennium B.C., more than 5,000 years ago. Fraternal interest groups began to promise defense in return for free food and other labors of women, children, and old men (Weber 1968; Paige and Paige 1981). Formal, differentiated military institutions such as armies soon emerged. Elsewhere, we show how military institutions first displayed women's structured subordination, separation of mind from hand work, the detailed division of labor, work for pay, and forms of discipline that mold the passions of men and, in response, of women (Hacker and Hacker 1987). These institutions continue to shape gender, eroticism, technology, and work.

Capitalist and socialist societies alike reflect this military heritage. No movement for gender equality or cooperative technology can afford to ignore the centrality of military institutions. Although many other forces mold both gender and technology, the effects of military institutions are as important as they are ignored. Military influence continues today, visible in social distance or antagonism between men and women, as well as in hierarchy and specialization in all major institutions. Here I am concerned with how military institutions constructed a kind of masculinity useful for them, and how this masculinity could be transmitted to young men through engineering education. As these men graduated and took their positions in state and industry, they shaped the labor process in part by what they were taught. One of today's great contradictions is between the primary purpose of these institutions and the large numbers of young women entering along with the men.

Engineering Education and Masculinity in Early Modern Europe

Early modern Europe saw the growth of ever larger states and armies, inseparable institutions. These, in turn, made trade and commerce possible on a scale before unknown, and stimulated tremendous growth of cities. Poor and landless farmers and unemployed city folk filled military ranks, as technological change "proletarianized" armies, allowing and demanding soldiers with less skill and equipment than before. Early modern armies themselves were much like traveling cities, often larger than the fixed towns they passed and at least as varied in their population (B. Hacker 1988; Childs 1982).

Women were a normal and vital part of these armies. Sometimes they fought, too, but mostly they were hard-working camp followers. They and the children often outnumbered the men, whose food and clothing they gathered and tended, whose health they protected, whose burdens they carried. The life was hard, as Barton Hacker (1981) observes, but better perhaps than poverty in a village or child labor in the fields at home. Probably more dangerous, it was also more exciting. Again, suggests Barton

Hacker (1988), these men and women likely enjoyed each other's company, perhaps more than those who governed would tolerate. Officials began excluding women from the march and sharply restricted the ratio of women to men. By the end of the nineteenth century, armies allowed no women at all, supply and other support functions having become bureaucratized military jobs filled only by men.

As early modern governments grew, so did the scope of civilian labor regulations. The state helped exclude women from civilian crafts (Howell 1986) as well as army life. But who then would staff burgeoning state and military institutions? The bureaucratic response was exclusively masculine (Ferguson 1984). Those in charge produced disciplined cadres of officers and state administrators, largely from institutions of engineering education. Engineering served as the technological arm of military institutions. Indeed, engineering was an exclusively military calling until the eighteenth century. The term *civil engineering* was coined for a new kind of practice not primarily concerned with weapons and fortifications. But the first engineering schools were military schools, which became the great polytechnics of western Europe (B. Hacker 1986).

The main purpose of the eighteenth-century engineering schools was to train the technical officers and administrators demanded by growing states and armies (Enroe 1981). Curricula fused technical training with cultural socialization that stressed hierarchy, discipline, loyalty, and self-control to a male-only student body (Hacker 1983a, 1986a). As graduates of these military schools became leaders in civilian society, they shaped organizations and institutions along military and thus patriarchal lines.

The church had largely lost to the state its control over education by the eighteenth century. A new and somewhat unruly elite displaced church and then aristocratic control over education. Science and mathematics supplanted theology and Latin. Important not only in themselves, mathematics and science served other functions in a rapidly changing world. One was the maintenance of gender stratification. The private, unpaid world of warmth and feeling was women's sphere. For young men, science and math lessons

61

promised to "cool the passions" and "calm the fires of youth" (Hacker 1983a). Youth, of course, meant male, and ever more often a young man from the unpredictable rising merchant classes. Thus another purpose of such courses, to "educate gentlemen, not to train mathematicians" (Enroe 1981).

Technical education, then as now, stabilized a form of patriarchal society during a period of rapid social and technological change, itself stimulated and shaped by the needs of states and armies. When military officers were no longer drawn from nobility alone, higher education served to mark the officer from the common soldier (Childs 1982). It also opened technical training to a wider range of men by providing an alternative to private apprenticeship.

West Point and the Military Model of U.S. Engineering Education

What these processes implied can be seen in the American experience. European models of engineering education had indeed proved that mathematics could discipline the mind as drill disciplined the body (Nenninger 1978). This was especially true in France. French formal engineering education itself began in the mid-eighteenth century. The primary purpose of cadet schools was to train and discipline the sons of the aristocracy for military and other state service. This proved too formidable a task, according to Ambrose (1966). The young nobles would not be "bridled." These early schools failed. The Ecole Militaire, and later the Ecole Polytechnic, proved more successful; the secret was rigid military discipline imposed on the student body. The new school gave France its best mathematicians, engineers, and officers. West Point, the first U.S. school of engineering, was modeled on the Ecole Polytechnic.

In West Point, the United States sought to provide a democratic institution of higher education based on utilitarian and scientific principles, rather than a classicist university emphasizing Greek, Latin, and moral philosophy. Jefferson, among others, felt such an institution would be more acceptable to the people in the form of a military academy than as a national university. West Point was founded on these principles in 1802. The experiment enjoyed little success during a chaotic first decade. But then Sylvanus Thayer arrived on the scene.

President Washington had sent Thayer to France for a close look at the Ecole Polytechnic. He returned with experience, methods, some faculty, and a thousand-volume technical library covering military art, cartography, engineering, and mathematics. More important for the present analysis, he introduced the reforms that came to bear his name, the Thayer system, which governed the academy for more than a century. Perceiving discipline as the root of the French military system, Thayer imposed a rigid military framework upon a student's every moment at the academy. Students entered a "novitiate, in which every man suffers equally, and every man is rewarded according to his performance, moving toward a common goal, under an impartial, impersonal command" (Dupuy 1958:4).

Initially, West Point cadets resisted the Thayer reforms. Possessing a strong sense of their rights, they often protested unpopular regulations on the lawn of an offending officer, whom they felt free to call "a scoundrel or a poltroon." But the new technology of education was effective in creating the new man. Thayer's method kept every cadet under constant observation and held him to strict, minimum rates of efficiency. West Point, like the Polytechnic, divided classes into small units, the better to observe and enforce discipline in daily activities. Students received grades every day and shifted from section to section each month according to their standing. Preparing study assignments was a military duty, with no excuses accepted (Dupuy 1958:6–9; Ambrose 1966).

Technical education everywhere in the early United States showed the pervasive influence of West Point. Faculty and graduates of the military academy found themselves welcome at other colleges and universities. One reason was their technical expertise. Of the 78 professorships they held in 1860, 40 were in mathematics, 16 in civil engineering. But teachers trained at West Point offered another benefit:

63

their familiarity with Thayer's system and its "rigid restrictions, departmentalized study and the supervision exercised over each individual student," which stood in "marked contrast to the generally lax discipline and grab-bag curricula of civilian institutions." The contrast was attractive to many of them. Dupuy (1958:14) continues, describing Thayer's direct and indirect "pedagogual insemination of the country" through the Thayer system and West Point graduates.

Undisciplined Harvard students found themselves under much tighter control in 1821. "The school at West Point," said George Ticknor as he revised both curriculum and student body management, "modeled after the most efficient of the high schools on the Continent, keeps the young men sent there in a state of intellectual discipline almost as active as is known anywhere in Europe." Following Thayer's example, Ticknor eliminated the long winter vacation, strictly enforced attendance, and curbed "extravagance" with limits on students' personal funds. Concerned about laxness in everything from entrance examinations to graduation, he urged rules "exacted with invarying strictness" to eliminate the unfit. None would be "indulged, or [enjoy] a great deal of idle time." Ticknor, like Thayer, stressed small sections, daily recitations by all students, monthly reclassification in divisions, and a published listing of all in order of merit. So successful was Ticknor that when President Monroe asked Thayer to work his magic at the University of Virginia, Thayer recommended applying the recent Harvard reforms, especially keeping the student occupied at all times (Dupuy 1958:15).

The West Point model also served America's growing passion for professionalism. Technical and engineering training and education were transformed in the nineteenth century (Sinclair 1974; Stine 1984; Calvert 1967). By the 1850s, a new technical elite had began to develop professional consciousness; engineering education was the most important factor in that process (Stine 1984). Distinguished by grades, tasks, titles, and income, engineers succeeded in separating themselves from the artisans, toolmakers, and inventors of the past. Their new social position depended heavily on degrees granted by the new technical institutions.

West Point transferred military models to industry as well as to education. Although early developments in business management were attributed to the advances and reforms achieved by the railroad industry, now we learn these 19th-century administrative innovations had military roots. O'Connell (1985) shows that cadres of West Point engineering graduates guided and directed these large-scale civilian projects. They introduced control procedures based on systematic bookkeeping and accounting, regulation by forms and inspection, all developed to meet military needs for ordering large numbers of men and large projects.

During the nineteenth century, military needs for "command" technologies fostered standardization and interchangeability of men and parts, for example in musket assembly (Hounshell 1984). A militarylike labor process spread throughout civilian industries. Employers attempted to govern workers' private lives and leisure habits as well, to be sure that they were sober and rested for work come Monday morning (Smith 1985). These innovations, like Taylorism, began in armories and weapon-producing industries and shops. Contracts then as now gave the persuasive edge to these innovations, favoring the entrepreneurs and shops that adapted to the military manner (Hounshell 1984; Smith 1985).

Patriarchal and military values of discipline, their structures of hierarchy and order, pervaded society through both education and industry. They provided a stable structure of gender stratification vis-à-vis technology, during times of rapid change in the eighteenth and then the nineteenth century. At each step along the way, technology and craft were redefined and women and minorities were discouraged or formally excluded, as in engineering education, vocational craft education, apprenticeships, and technical and craft training in the military. In late nineteenth-century America the middle class displayed "an unprecedented enthusiasm for its own . . . devices for self-improvement." Middle-class men could achieve identity through profession, with no need for community support or rigid class barriers as in Europe. Ambitious men "were instrumental in structuring society according to a distinct vision—the vertical one of career," comments Bledstein (1976:ix).

Competition, merit, and especially discipline and control defined both masculinity and success for the upwardly mobile young man. Discipline helped the man express a kind of creativity, but also strengthened his belief in authority and in education as the basis for achievement and success. The schools that provided this opportunity in the mid-nineteenth century had borrowed heavily from West Point's example. Failure was double-edged: the system required a certain ratio of failures to successes, but refused to condone failure in any man. Bledstein shows that men defined failure in new terms—not to realize one's potential, not to make the grade, to waste one's energy in disrespectable and disorderly behavior. At West Point, in particular, men experienced failure as humiliation, mortification, disgrace (Fleming 1969). Education need not coercively control young men's behavior and emotions; it need only help them do it to themselves, a much more efficient approach.

Failure was, and is, a constant experience in engineering education. At mid-nineteenth-century West Point failure rates hovered around 50 to 60 percent, equal to or higher than other military schools (Morrison 1970:183–185). Harvard, Columbia, Princeton, and other colleges shared the flunk-out norms of the military academies, viewing "themselves as character-builders and disciplinarians of the mind first, and purveyors of knowledge second" (Morrison 1970: 182–183). Mathematics teaching and testing continued to perform the weeding function suggested in earlier debates (Hacker 1983a), accounting for 72 percent of midcentury West Point failures. It became the first subject rationalized for evaluation through paper-and-pencil testing, rather than fieldwork, projects, or other displays of physical accomplishment (Cardwell 1957). Testing was, of course, much cheaper.

Early Twentieth-Century Trends

Military institutions dominated the reform of engineering education in early twentieth-century America (Noble 1977). During World War I the U.S. Army mounted research programs to test large batches of men and allocate them to specific jobs and tasks. Elaborate systems of testing and grading leading to job placement became the basis for postwar curricular reforms in higher education. Military-inspired and university-perfected job definitions and training proved of great benefit to industries. They had long struggled to solve the problems of measuring skills and allocating workers to carefully defined and specified jobs. This process—school-tested distribution to hierarchically ranked and specialized jobs in industry—spread to secondary schools. This pattern further strengthened that arid technical rationality built on suppressed emotion decried earlier by critical theorists and radical feminists. That peculiar form of rationality was captured as a core ingredient of the identity for the ideal middle-class white man. For the working class, masculinized programs like vocational crafts education until recently excluded girls by law and custom.

There was, however, some concern about all this testing and grading. Engineering educators such as Charles Mann could not be sure if good grades predicted good engineers. What, he wondered, did getting good grades mean? But Mann did more than wonder whether or not industry was getting the best engineering talent through this method of school testing. His research led him to publish the first U.S. study of engineering education (Mann 1918).

In one project, he evaluated the engineering graduate by compiling an index of several academic measures: high school math, English, and physics scores; freshman grades in English, math, and chemistry; peer ratings of intelligence, judgments of teachers, and scores on some 15 tests of academic ability, largely math and science. Those with high scores on these measures did indeed graduate with honors, while those who scored low failed more than half their subjects and dropped out. The best correlations with this composite score were results from one supply-the-missing-word test and results from five mathematics exams. Curiously, Mann noted eight scores that had correlated not at all with the composite score: reading, vocabulary, opposites of words, physics lab problems, matching diagrams with sentences, completing imperfect diagrams, physics problems stated in words, and construction of mechanical devices from unassembled parts. Many of these seem peculiarly necessary to what one understands as good engineering. In another project, Mann found further reason to doubt academic measures. Employer ratings of the skills, ingenuity, and productivity of engineering school graduates yielded no correlation at all with their previous college grades.

Recently I asked the dean of an East Coast engineering school if this question persists. Do good grades necessarily forecast a good engineer? As a matter of fact, he said, a graduate student recently checked this very school. Taking alumni contributions as a very loose measure of success, or "good engineering," he did indeed, for the first time, find a significant statistical correlation between grades and engineering "ability" so measured. But the correlation was negative—the lower the grades, the greater the contribution and presumed success. Essentially, getting good grades meant—and means, as I observed in today's classroom—that one could pass the tests.

By the late nineteenth century, school culture had replaced shop culture and the apprentice system as a way of turning young men into engineers. In the first decades of the twentieth century, courses in mathematics, science, and economics further displaced shop, political science, history, and foreign languages; evaluation continued to shift from projects and hands-on interaction with physical tools and materials to paper-and-pencil tests. These trends truly worried Mann. Handiwork seemed to him significant for engineers, but too many students were being weeded out by grades, primarily in mathematics.

Subsequent engineering education reports in the 1920s and 1930s showed less of Mann's intense curiosity, more of the bureaucrat's concern for turf—whether, for instance, schools of engineering or ROTC units should teach the accredited courses. Concerns about income also flourished. Too many engineers would depress salaries, and elite eastern schools complained about the large land-grant colleges springing up across the country. Engineering graduates were described as "products," the dropouts as "by-products" (Wickenden 1930–1934:1078). Advocates of the American way rejected some aspects of the elite European system that allowed only a few to enter engineering school. They preferred giving each young man the "chance" to achieve what he could.

In a comparative study of European and U.S. engineering education, Wickenden noted that Great Britain retained the links between engineer and craftsman to promote vertical mobility. The French, however, had first perceived the need for a scientifically trained elite corps of engineers for the higher ranks. Private schools still selected on the basis of fairly simple examinations, but state-run institutions pioneered much more rigorous systems of examination, systems that in the United States reduced the proportion of "foreigners" in the student body (Wickenden 1930–1934:18).

While British and Scottish models continued to develop career ladders in the technical occupations from shop floor to engineer, Germany, France, and the United States moved toward distinct layers of schools with different levels of, and in time degrees for, certified skill. It was thought "wasteful to teach mechanics science and handicrafts . . . like teaching soldiers strategy" (Wickenden 1930–1934:42).

Wickenden represented the concern for organization of the technical work force and its interface with industry, military, and society in general. The country ought to have a large number of young men with some training in the technical disciplines, he thought, whether or not they graduated. And maintaining the sense of upward mobility through engineering, a traditional route for working-class boys, was also a good idea. Only later did the beneficent role of community colleges emerge, to keep a lid on aspirations (Pincus 1980). With a mere two-year degree, one does not expect so much.

Wickenden's report is a classic statement of military methods applied to engineering instruction. It helps us understand why it is not mathematics so much as the math-based professions that discourage women:

> Engineering education reflects our national genius for quantity production. Pressed to get a maximum result in a minimum of time, engineering educators have borrowed, half unconsciously, from the management methods of industry. The essence of the scheme consists in first visualizing the process as a whole, then dividing it into major steps in a logical progression and finally breaking the work down into small units to be done in a definite sequence, under prearranged conditions and with the materials supplied precisely when needed and in the most convenient form, the task sequence to be carried out under close supervision, with continuous inspection and grading of piece parts, and the rewards to be paid in terms of a standard task with quality bonus. (Wickenden 1930–34:109)

Ironically, Wickenden attributed these processes to American manufacturing, rather than to the military production systems where they originated. This was one of the deliberate attempts to downplay for public consumption the extent of military influence on technical education (Noble 1977).

Contemporary Changes in Gender and Labor Process

In Chapter 3, I described how an outsider felt as a part of the engineering student body. In this chapter I have sketched a picture of military institutions—the central all-male institutions that made the state possible—shaping engineering education, defining a hierarchy of masculinities. These are antithetical to democratic cooperation. Underlying this system is stratification based on gender and on the masculine definition of both technology and eroticism that allows patriarchal institutions to persist and flourish. Military and related institutions such as engineering schools came ultimately to stabilize or redefine a kind of masculinity when questions of gender and technology arose. Engineering's continuing symbiotic relationship with military institutions affects the shape of work and education as much today as ever.

Paradoxically, engineering today appears to be opening to women. In the last 20 years, the percentage of B.S. degrees in engineering awarded to women has risen from 4 to 14 percent. Computer sciences, a new field, has a better record yet. Even while this occurs, however, as the case of AT&T would suggest, new and primarily military-stimulated technologies such as computer-aided design (CAD) routinize or automate many engineering functions (Edwards 1986a, 1986b, forthcoming). Cooley (1986) poignantly describes the "Taylorization" of engineering in Great Britain, as engineers work shifts at a pace impossible for the man who has been around a few years. National Science Foundation surveys report engineers increasingly fear employment difficulties ahead. They see less chance to do creative work and greater likelihood of working under factory like conditions. (NSF 1982, 1984a, 1984b).

Places in engineering school are harder to come by, even with a bloated military budget—the main variable in statistical models predicting engineering "manpower" needs. Grade requirements for entry and retention rise. Administrators say all this is to "raise the quality" of the engineering students. They may, as my experience suggests, even believe this. At the same time, to the dismay of the engineering profession, technicians are hired in the place of engineers, and women and minorities are encouraged to apply (Braverman 1974; Hacker and Starnes 1983). Meanwhile, the money and the middle-class white men are drawn by innovative and seemingly limitless research and development opportunities at the graduate level and in the laboratories.

Military influence is not found only in higher education. The largest vocational and technical training institutions in the United States belong to the armed forces; the federal budget for military education is larger than that for nonmilitary higher education (Gillman 1983). Military education includes vocational and other specifically military training, the on-base courses around the world, ROTC programs, and programs at war colleges and elite academies. It also includes the indirect influence of military institutions of higher education with which we tend to be more familiar, although there are still surprises. Recently I attended a national conference on adult education where, I was told, 60 percent of registrants' fees had been paid by the military. The relationship between military institutions and education, particularly technical education, should be obvious.

And so we have come full circle. Extensive military regimen in daily life, with frequent and grueling examinations, teaches students obedience to hierarchical forms of discipline. Such methods also teach repression, as one contemporary mathematics professor has observed (Davis 1980). When asked about the value of these tests, another replied that they "show you can do it." But women are showing they can perform as well as men on these criteria. This will not mean greater equality, if history is any guide. Since a large part of the definition of masculinity lies in superiority to women, the criteria will change.

Weber (1968), as noted earlier, saw military discipline as the model for all discipline, affecting the state, the economy, and the family. State and patriarchal family therefore need each other, enough reason to question the existence of either. Like Mumford, Weber dealt here and there with the control of sexuality as a driving force behind social organization. But both have left it for others to find the links among military institutions, authoritarian technics, and being a woman or a man.

This is truly another time of change in gender and technology, and we can act in effective ways. Military institutions are not the only source of patriarchal stability, but they have long been its most reliable support. Alternatives to capital, state, and family, furthermore, exist only in partial and not very widely observed forms. In the second part of this book I use the Mondragon system of industrial cooperatives as a case study to explore conditions of workplace democracy, gender equality, and the organization of technology in cooperative society. To the extent that these alternative models still maintain gender hierarchy, we have more work to do. Not all things are possible; at certain times, one can make only limited gains. But that is what life can be about.

PART II

Mondragon: Gender, Technology, and Power in Cooperative Workplaces

CHAPTER 5

Cooperativism:
Principles and Practice

The experiences reported in Chapter 4 can suggest many paths to take. I learned that to understand gender and technology we must also study the influence of military institutions in our workplaces, in engineering education, and in our everyday erotic lives. In this and the next chapter I look at a particular kind of workplace and at related technical education. Cooperative workplaces offer a contrast to militarylike organization of work. They provide potential sites of peace conversion activity (Melman 1987). They can declare that all members are workers, all workers are members, with one vote each. They can jointly decide what to make or sell and how, share most of the profits, and give the rest back to the community for child care, health, and education. They might rotate management positions; they might choose directors by lot, to maximize the sharing of skills and information. Cooperative workplaces could also require gender equality and a nonhierarchical administrative apparatus.

We shall see there have been three waves of cooperativism in the United States. Nineteenth- and early 20th-century cooperatives sprang from labor unrest, and were eventually demolished by the powers that be—banks, corporations, the state. The federal government sponsored cooperatives in the 1930s to avoid labor unrest during the Depression. These cooperatives failed when support was withdrawn. In the 1960s structural changes in society and widespread loss of faith and interest in the dominant culture produced yet another wave of cooperative workplaces. In many of the radical cooperatives of the nineteenth century, and those of the 1960s, control over technology, democratic participation, and gender mutuality were central workplace concerns.

75

A Brief History of Cooperativism

Modern cooperatives began to appear in numbers in the late eighteenth and early nineteenth centuries, primarily along with the industrial transformation of English society. Times of significant change are hardest on those with least power (Thompson 1963), and hard times are one of the inspirations for cooperation. Women have least power in every class, caste, or stratum.[1] Perhaps the location of women at the lower levels of the social structure in part explains our attraction to cooperativism. This and other aspects of women's condition emerge from the history of women in the movement for cooperative organizations.

There may have been little difference between the lives of British men and those of British women at the end of the eighteenth century. The countryside was impoverished from the burden of what many perceived to be a bloated military. Both men and women faced starvation and further loss of jobs through mechanization. Luddites smashed the machines that destroyed their livelihood in the textile industry; Parliament enacted the death penalty for anyone so rash. Attacking this law in the House of Lords, Lord Byron pictured a country suffering "from a double infliction of an idle military and a starving population" (Peel 1968:73). England's long struggle against French imperial pretensions precipitated the trouble, according to Frank Peel:

> To crush Napoleon we had not only sent our own armies, but we had also in our pay all the hordes of the despots of Europe. Truly it was a revolting and humiliating spectacle. The hard-earned money wrung from our own working people, till they rose in their misery, and even threatened king and government with destruction, went to be divided among a host of despots and slaves. (Peel 1968:23)

Drawing on a rich oral tradition, Peel in the late nineteenth century described conditions earlier in the century: commerce in shambles, food prices soaring, bankruptcies in the thousands. Children cried for food, and "gaunt famine-stricken crowds took to the streets demanding bread.

Meanwhile, "manufacturers everywhere were availing themselves of the many wonderful inventions that were being brought out for cheapening labour." Workers, if better educated, says Peel, might "have known it was their duty to lie down in the nearest ditch and die . . . in order that the march of progress might not be delayed or obstructed." Rather, "they resolved in their ignorance to destroy" the machinery that threw thousands out of work (Peel 1968:24–25). Thus, control over the organization of work and technological change had become central themes for these radical worker and community actions.

Scores of Luddites were shot or hanged, Peel reports from the journal of Quaker Thomas Shillito, who, with friends, made the rounds of homes of widows and bereaved parents, of magistrate and informer alike. The Quakers listened, healed the wounds of community, arranged for leniency in some cases, and began to organize for collective responsibility of widows and orphans. Indeed, in Berrisfield, several surviving remnants of families had already gathered to live together (Peel 1968:272–282).

Hundreds of workers and consumer cooperatives sprang up in England, Europe, and the United States, from the 1790s on (Rozwenc 1975). The history of the United States differed greatly from that of Europe, as this country determined not to relive the grim path of industrialization in England and the Continent. Yet parallels in history do exist, as do parallels in movements for cooperativism.

Women worked with manufacturer and revolutionary visionary Robert Owen in England, and, after 1825, in the United States, to help found "new society" cooperatives such as New Harmony in Indiana. Gender mutuality and a liberated eroticism were as significant issues among these libertarian socialists as was democracy in the workplace (Kimmel 1987).

During the 1840s in England, out-of-work farmers, craftspeople, and factory workers, often centered by women, formed producer co-ops. State and industry leaders met these efforts with force and violence. They imprisoned or deported many workers, and killed others. Given this opposition to producer or worker co-ops, in 1844 Ann Tweedale and other blacklisted weavers organized consumers to purchase food, clothing, and other necessities at more reasonable prices than otherwise available (Giese 1982).

This co-op, the Rochdale Pioneers, developed practical principles for a consumer co-op—one member, one vote; operation by cash, not credit; return on investment set at bank interest rates; set-asides for education and development; and, after these and expenses, the remainder of the profits or surplus was returned to patrons as a percentage of their purchase. The Rochdale Pioneers saw cooperativism as one step toward a larger goal, a socialist society characterized by economic democracy. Rochdale has served as a model for many other co-ops in England, the United States, and Europe, including Mondragon.

In the eighteenth and early nineteenth centuries, rural England was still being pushed from the land as it had for centuries, but it was also being drawn by factory work. Grim and grinding though such work was, it might still seem more appealing than work on the land. A letter by "the late Mrs. Burrows" describes "A Childhood in the Fens About 1850–1860" (in Davies 1975:109–114)

> On the day that I was eight years of age, I left school, and began to work fourteen hours a day in the fields, with from forty to fifty other children of whom, even at that early age, I was the eldest. We were followed all day long by an old man carrying a long whip in his hand which he did not forget to use. (Davies 1975:109)

The children left the town at 6:00 a.m., walking often five miles to the field, returning after dark.

> In all the four years I worked in the fields, I never worked one hour under cover of a barn, and only once did we have a meal in a house. . . . Had I time I could write how our gang of children, one winter's night, had to wade for half a mile through the flood. . . . For four years, summer and winter, I worked in these gangs—no holidays of any sort, with the exception of very wet days and Sundays—and at the end of that time it felt like Heaven to me when I was taken to the town of Leeds, and put to work in the factory. (Davies 1975:110, 112)

Life as We Have Known It, by Co-operative Working Women (Davies 1975) originally published in 1931, reproduces letters such as these from women workers on the significance of the Women's Cooperative Guild of England, founded in 1883. The conditions under which many of the women lived and worked were impossibly difficult, as Mrs. Burrows testifies. Household technology, such as heat and plumbing, and issues of sexual harassment at work concerned these women of resistance. Some tell of a precarious existence as servant or clerk, and all too great a chance of being raped by one's employer. Some gained a degree of independence as nurse or midwife. Many speak of rounds of childbirth and illness, of days of hunger for themselves and their families, of caring for husbands injured or ill from working in the mines.

Yet, as Virginia Woolf imagines in her introduction to this work, "'the poor,' 'the working classes,' or by whatever name you choose to call them, are not downtrodden, envious and exhausted; they are humorous and vigorous and thoroughly independent" (Woolf 1975:xxvii). They read what they could come across, argued, imagined, and began to question. Guild meetings would seem to have required more time or energy than anyone could muster, yet these reports help us understand how some of the most creative efforts can occur in the worst of times. True, the guild stores offered lower prices. As important in these accounts, however, were the books, conversations, and meetings that offered a different idea to keep the mind alive for one more week, as one put it. In Woolf's words,

> It was then, I suppose, sometime in the eighties, that the Women's Guild crept modestly and tentatively into existence. For a time it occupied an inch or two of space in the *Co-operative News* which called itself The Women's Corner. It was there that Mrs. Acland asked, "Why should we not hold our Co-operative mothers' meetings, when we may bring our work and sit together, one of us reading some Cooperative work aloud, which may afterwards be discussed?" And on April 18th, 1883, she announced that the Women's Guild now numbered seven members. It was the Guild then that drew to itself all that restless wishing and dreaming. It was the Guild that made a central meeting place where formed and solidified all that was else so scattered and incoherent. . . . It gave them in the first place the rarest of all possessions—a room where they could sit down and think remote from boiling saucepans and crying children. (Woolf 1975):xxxv-xxxvi)

79

It was the Guild's practice to combine education with action. Davies and others saw "co-operation" not "as a thrift movement," but "the beginning of a great revolution" based on the "desire to see the Community in control, instead of the Capitalists." They said "money is like muck, no good unless it is spread" and hoped to see that "capital becomes the tool of labour and not its master" (Davies 1975:ix-x). Woolf described what happened as Guild

> membership grew, and twenty or thirty women made a practice of meeting weekly, so their ideas increased, and their interests widened. Instead of discussing merely their own taps and their own sinks and their own long hours and little pay, they began to discuss education and taxation and the conditions of work in the country at large. The women . . . learnt to speak out, boldly and authoritatively, about every question of civic life . . . asking not only for baths and wages and electric light, but also for adult suffrage and the taxation of land values and divorce law reform. Thus in a year or two they were to demand peace and disarmament and the spread of Co-operative principles, not only among the working people of Great Britain, but among the nations of the world. (Woolf 1975:xxxvi)

Meetings provided information on poor laws, books, education in labor affairs, worker travel and tours, involvement in women's suffrage, and, in the early twentieth century, international work for disarmament. The women report learning to "speak boldly even at Men's Meetings" and how the Guild "brought new visions and opened the doors and the windows." At its 1930 conference, with delegates from over 20 countries, the Guild continued to argue for both co-operative workplaces and international disarmament (Davies 1974:xiii).

The same movement that in France gave birth to Fourier and in England to Robert Owen stimulated the development of cooperatives in New England (Bemis 1888). Powerful among these efforts was the Protective Union Store Movement of the 1840s–1860s (Rozwenc 1975). Co-ops surged in the economic crises of the late nineteenth century. In 1886, Imogen C. Fales founded the Sociological Society of America to unfold "the great cooperative results of the Central Coöperative Board of the U.K." and began to publish an American version of *The Coöperative News* (Bemis 1888:105–106).

Agrarian alliances such as the Patrons of Husbandry (Grange), the more political Farmer's Alliances, and the People's Party emerged from a massive cooperative movement of millions of Americans. The agrarian movement developed a powerful culture of rural resistance to the emerging corporate state (Goodwyn 1975). Large demonstrations, wagon trains of families, protested banking and finance practices of capitalism. Picnics and other outings gathered thousands in the heartland, the South and West. They argued for people's control over the banks and financial system of the country, a system grinding them into the dust through the crop lien system. Black and white farmers and sharecroppers sometimes overcame their structured separateness, but cooperative efforts that crossed racial lines were particular targets of attack (Woodward 1971). Black cooperatives were the more impressive, given the life-threatening nature of cooperation at the time.

The rise of the corporate state, with its centralized and hierarchical finance structure, spelled the end of the last great agrarian revolt. Goodwyn (1975) suggests women were more prominent in this agrarian movement for cooperation than the histories, his included, would indicate. "The evidence is both tantalizing in implication and difficult to gather." He lists a number of women for future study, such as Mary Elizabeth Lease of Kansas, whose "famous injunction to farmers to 'raise less corn and more hell!'" echoes yet (Goodwyn 1975:339).

White ethnic urban populations created their own forms of cooperative structures, such as the fraternal benefit societies that insured against the loss of the male breadwinner. Women, in other words, were the largest group of people excluded from membership. With an increasing number of single women in communities and workplaces, some created independent "fraternal" benefit societies for women, such as the Polish Women's Alliance of 1898. Its goals have a distinctive feminist character, although cast in terms of strengthening "national culture and the family" (Radzialowski 1978).

Perhaps the best known of the worker cooperatives of the late nineteenth century, however, were those of the Knights of Labor. They organized many producer and consumer cooperatives in city and country alike. Women were active in these cooperative efforts, particularly in the textile industry. The Martha Washington Coöperative Association, for example, in which "all the officers are women," banded together "for the manufacture of overalls, shirts and knit goods" (Warner 1888:421). In 1886, women workers in an Illinois clothing factory thought they had permission to take off work for a labor parade. The employer said otherwise, and locked them out. "Being afterwards blacklisted" they wrote, "It became a question of coöperation or starve." Our Girls' Coöperative Clothing Manufacturing Company later affiliated with the Knights of Labor to purchase twenty machines, bypassing subcontractors to produce ready-made clothing on their own (Warner 1888:421).

At the same time, women networked and organized nationally as well. Twelve women and six men, some victimized for their labor activities in the Knights of Labor, created one of the first western consumer co-ops. The Fannie Allyn Coöperative Association circulated a bulletin throughout the country for an 1886 co-op fair in Cincinnati. "Believing that our only salvation lies in coöperation . . . we therefore, having full confidence in each other, make a bold attempt in forming a coöperative concern" (Warner 1888: 402). The fair was a smashing success. Virtually all co-op enterprises in the country sent goods for exhibit and raffle. The result "was to put the coöperative enterprise on a sound financial basis, and to give coöperators in different parts of the country a better appreciation of each other's work" (Warner 1888:402).

Both worker and farmer movements were to falter in part on credit withheld or denied, despite amassing capital reserves in land and equipment, and in promised crops. Private corporations undersold cooperative stores, refused the sale of seed and equipment, and blacklisted cooperative members and agents. By century's end, the Knights of Labor "coop stores and factories had been burned out, bombed out, wrecked by company agents, forced out economically, or abandoned" (Giese 1982:322). Early twentieth-century efforts like that of Illinois United Mine Workers met a similar fate. Other cooperatives, operating within less revolutionary frames, such as the Pacific Northwest's plywood cooperatives (Berman 1967) and the many consumer co-ops indistinguishable from any large chain store, survive today (Kravitz 1974).

The cooperativism of nineteenth and early twentieth centuries stemmed largely from labor unrest. A second wave of producer cooperatives crested amid massive unemployment in the Depression years of the 1930s. In contrast to the grassroots efforts of the past, the federal government stimulated and funded their formation (Jackall and Levin 1984). The government clearly intended these cooperatives as a stop-gap measure to employ the "unemployable" and to calm potential unrest due to economic crisis. Even under these conditions, their performance was remarkable, perhaps most of all in the labor-intensive, female-dominated industries. (See Jones and Schneider 1984 for an intricate study of the economistic data gathered from the California co-ops of this era.)

announced it would retain ownership of co-op assets rather than distribute these among the members, that it would retain control over appointment of managers, and that it would make decisions on production quotas. Thereafter, members' dedication to cooperative principles declined. In 1939 state support ceased. Such short-term commitment, among other problems, spelled the demise of most efforts. Rothschild and Whitt (1986) describe the state's attitude toward Depression co-ops as one of indifference or neglect, except in the case of farmer's cooperatives. With stronger and consistent state support, the farmers' coops flourished. As these and other authors note, cooperativism can be perceived as a "third way," an economic form of organization that avoids the worst evils of both capitalism and state socialism. But both capitalist and socialist governments are uneasy with cooperatives, because they compete with both private and state enterprise. The latest versions of workplace democracy, however, show few signs of challenging technology or gender inequality.

Third-wave cooperativism in the United States is best represented by the thousand small collective ventures begun in the 1960s and 1970s, now flourishing in such congenial settings as San Francisco, Boston, Eugene, Minneapolis, Austin, and Ann Arbor (Jackall and Crain 1984). Almost half the co-ops sampled in a recent study by Jackall and Crain (1984) are in food-related businesses. Members are young, college educated, white, and 61 percent female. Modern co-ops emphasize a technology compatible with the environment and with democratic participation (Hartzell 1987).

This wave of cooperativism, unlike the first, which was characterized by labor radicalism, or the second-wave Depression-inspired co-ops of the 1930s, grew from revolutionary ideology and practice—a rejection of major American institutions and their system of values. As in the first wave, there is again a critical analysis of control over technology, of the effects of military institutions on economy and everyday life, and of tender relations. These cooperatives are best seen as a "youthful revolt in this century against the cultural and social consequences of the triumph of industrial capitalism" (Jackall and Crain 1984:95). But why so high a proportion of women?

First, food-related businesses fit with traditional skills of women. But also "feminism has placed a premium on group cooperation and camaraderie among women, and on doing work with political implications." Cooperatives, like feminism, emphasize "self-reliance and initiative." Further, in co-ops, women can earn as much as men and can learn such formerly men-only skills as carpentry and truck driving (Jackall and Crain 1984:95).

"Socialist islands in a capitalist sea," or "small outposts, bastions of socialist virtue and practice, in a hostile environment," many don't survive, but burn out in "histories of noble failure" (Jackall and Crain 1984:101–102). The successes are noteworthy for their suppleness, their organizational flexibility to adapt within the non-cooperative larger society. Hal Hartzell (1987) of the Eugene, Oregon, tree-planting Hoedads, credits the participation of women for the Hoedads' successful encounter with the demands of face-to-face cooperation and conflict inherent in cooperative organization and with the need for technical innovation.

Today, current economic crises stimulate a new round of profit-sharing efforts such as employee stock ownership plans

(ESOPs; see Rosen et al. 1986). These efforts are supported both by the Reagan administration and by labor unions, though not for the same reasons. ESOPs have problems. Some suspect management merely wants to transfer responsibility for benefits to workers or to receive newly legislated tax and interest breaks for jointly owned firms. Many ESOPs arise because of the tendency for plants to shut down and move overseas for cheaper labor. Workers buy out the firm, hoping to make it viable once again. Rothschild and Whitt (1986) find that few ESOPs allow much worker participation in decisions about how the work should be done. Control, rather than ownership per se, seems to be of crucial importance. Other ESOP ventures are more fruitful, particularly when workers own, and can vote, the majority of stock. These ESOPs represent about 10 per cent of the total (Rosen et al. 1986).

As ESOPs increase in number, so do other innovative attempts to combine capitalist with cooperative enterprise or to convert traditional to democratic workplaces. Bernstein (1982) and Lindenfeld and Rothschild-Whitt (1982) locate firms along a continuum, from the most traditional, bureaucratically controlled and privately owned firms, which "may provide a suggestion box for workers," to the fully worker-owned and -controlled Mondragon cooperatives. The president of one large U.S. insurance company is transferring his company to worker control to create "an environment where each member of the community has the opportunity to grow and develop in his or her own unique way, to self-actualize" (Zwerdling 1982:225). The object is not self-management itself, but maximizing humanness. In another instance, workers of a high-tech electronics firm were faced with changing market conditions and a concomitant change in the structure of the organization. Management, wanting to increase production supervisory capacities and effectiveness, constructed a cooperative parallel structure within and alongside the traditional organization (Kanter et al. 1982).

Philosophy and Structure of
Workplace Cooperatives

Although many cooperators cite their debt to Marxist theory, in fact the centralizing tendencies suggested by Marx contradict the grass-roots type of participatory democracy. Participatory democracy is rooted in the works of Rousseau, John Stuart Mill, and others who argued that a participatory polity was impossible without other participatory institutions (Rothschild and Whitt 1986; Pateman 1970). The intellectual foundations of cooperativism are also rooted in social anarchism, the vision of workers' cooperatives and communities linked in democratic federation without need for bureaucratic state control. Insistence on local and participatory democracy against centralized organization led anarchists to split from Marxists in the nineteenth century, a division characteristic of socialist movements ever since (Rothschild and Whitt 1986). Social anarchists have thought deeply about means and ends.

> Anarchist strategies stress the congruence of means and ends, and thus, for example, would not propose mandatory organizations to reeducate people for a free society. They would not advocate violent means to achieve a peaceful society; nor would they choose centralized means to attain a decentralized society. From the congruence of means and ends flows the conception of "direct action." Direct actions are directly relevant to the ends sought and are based on individual decisions as to whether or not to participate in the proposed action. Examples of direct action include the general strike, resistance to the draft, and the creation of food cooperatives, credit unions, and worker-run workplaces. (Rothschild and Whitt 1986:17)

The above quote illustrates some of the philosophical and historical roots of the movement for cooperation, as it is called.

Industrial cooperatives, for many reasons, attract attention from a growing international body of social scientists, managers, and workers (see Berman 1967; Pateman 1970; Bernstein 1982; Vanek 1977; Oakeshott 1978; Lindenfeld and Rothschild-Whitt 1982; Fusfield 1983; Derber and Schwartz 1983; Jackall and Levin 1984; Jansson and

Hellmark 1986). Economic crises persuade workers to buy out failing or runaway firms in an attempt to save jobs and community. Political movements, as in Sweden, emphasize greater worker participation in decision-making and profits. Italy's parties of the left support cooperativism. In the United States the rallying cry becomes "labor capitalism" (Rosen et al. 1986).

Industrial cooperatives are workplaces owned and managed in varying degrees by the workers themselves, where "labor hires capital" rather than the reverse. Some see them as a peaceful route to a democratic and socialist society; others seek a bulwark against socialism, preserving elements of capitalism against a slide into state ownership and control of business and industry (Giese 1982). But many hail cooperatives as a "third way," an alternative to the problems of both monopoly capitalism (e.g., runaway capital, widespread unemployment) and authoritarian socialism (e.g., lack of dynamism or autonomy at work).

Rothschild and Whitt (1986) provide the most comprehensive theoretical framework for the analysis of cooperatives. In an earlier analysis, Rothschild-Whitt (1982) also extended Weber's discussion of organizational authority to democratic organizations. Weber (1968) recognized only three sources of authority: tradition, charismatic leadership, or legal-rational bureaucracy. But Rothschild-Whitt stresses a fourth type of organization, one taking its authority democratically from consensus hammered out in the group itself.

Rothschild and Whitt (1986) offer examples of cooperatives working from consensus for the basis of authority, in free schools, radical newspapers, and other new institutions of the 1960s. The process of continuing a discussion, rather than voting down a minority, seems inefficient in the short run, but over time the encouragement to take part allows more individual creativity and support for the group effort. These efforts require full community and cultural support within larger cooperatives, especially those with sophisticated technologies. We return to this problem later.

The problems of co-op survival in a capitalist market are many: a system of law that is hostile to or poorly equipped to deal with cooperatives (Ellerman 1982); becoming profitable and selling out; a tendency to take higher wages rather than reinvest sufficiently; being "co-opted" or forced out by traditional interests; lack of support systems in marketing and planning, investment, and the like; buying an already failing firm; hiring nonmembers at lower wages; being long on vision and short on know-how, or the reverse; common ownership without control. The Mondragon cooperatives have devised structures and processes that illustrate counter-practices successful even within a capitalist market.

Rothschild and Whitt (1986) analyze seven dimensions other than consensus along which bureaucratic organizations diverge from collective, or cooperative. Cooperatives, unlike bureaucratic organizations, disdain formal rules and deal with each situation on its own ethical terms. Social control rests on moral appeal to like-minded members, not formal law. Community rather than impersonality defines social relations. Friends with shared values informally assess each other's knowledge and skills rather than rely on specialized training and credentials. Solidarity and group welfare come before material incentives. Differences between workers fade as they share skills and sometimes rotate tasks. Expertise is demystified as much as possible.

Several factors promote cooperation. Within the co-op, no one should expect a job to last forever, but only so long as it's needed. Membership must be limited to ensure participation, and workers must share values and be willing to give and take criticism from their peers and themselves. Specialized knowledge must be demystified and widely shared. To cope with the world outside the co-op takes a set of values and services clearly alternative to those of the dominant community, support rather than direction from relevant professional communities, and a social movement orientation (Rothschild and Whitt 1986).

Other students of worker cooperatives offer their own practical and analytic guidelines. Bernstein (1982) defines three dimensions for evaluating worker participation: (1) the degree of *control* employees enjoy over any particular decision (from suggestion box to workers' groups superior to management); (2) the *issues* over which control is exercised (from pay to choice of product, distribution of profits, organization of work, and selection of managers); and (3) the organizational *level* at which their control is exercised (from minor job enrichment of tasks to managerial prerogatives at the top).

Analyzing eighty studies of work democratization—in the United States, Great Britain, Norway, Israel, Czechoslovakia, Spain, West Germany, Belgium, Yugoslavia, Sweden, China, Algeria, the Soviet Union, and Canada—Bernstein (1982) suggests five elements necessary for minimal workplace democracy:

(1) employee access to, and sharing of, management-level information
(2) guaranteed protection of employee from reprisal for voicing criticism
(3) an independent board of appeals to settle disputes between those holding managing positions and those being managed
(4) a particular set of attitudes and values (cooperative)
(5) frequent return to participating employees of at least a portion of the surplus they produce (above their regular wages)

Gunn (1984) adds the dimension of race and gender to class, and the oppositional or resistance community context necessary for the full functioning of democratic workplaces. Although some evidence exists that women's gender training yields better talents for cooperation (Rothschild 1987), not all women's groups are cooperative any more than all cooperatives are gender mutual. We cannot here as anywhere depend on gender alone. In most all of this contemporary analytic material, the organization of technology and traditional gender relations (e.g., in the family) are accepted as given.

Much of the literature on cooperativism prides itself on being "hard-nosed," pragmatic, economistic. Perhaps this offsets the notion of "bread-baking hippies sitting in a circle staring at a candle," as one of my students described cooperatives. Scholars emphasize efficiency and productivity, sometimes even worker satisfaction, compared with capitalist firms. They tend to ignore such "soft" subjects as gender stratification, ecology, and the shape of technology. In response to the deemphasis on gender, Joan Acker (1982) speaks to this international body of scholars dedicated to workplace democracy:

> In principle, democracy, which implies equality of participation in decision-making, does not exist when large numbers of people who are affected by decisions have no part in their formulation. . . . Sexual equality, in this sense, is logically necessary for democracy in working life. To argue that sexual equality is not necessary for work-life democracy is to argue for the continuation of the male monopoly of decision-making power, essentially to argue against democracy. (p. i)

Feldberg (1981) warns, however, that if cooperativism is introduced with little concern for women's participation, this could further consolidate men's power in the workplace and weaken that of women.

We enjoy excellent feminist analyses of the role of women workers in capitalist and socialist systems, but know little of gender stratification within cooperatives or how it affects relationships between co-ops and in their larger communities (for exception, see Davies 1975; Johnson 1978; Feldberg 1981; Acker 1982; Schlesinger and Bart 1982; Wajcman 1983; Pateman 1983). No work has yet addressed gender stratification or the organization of technology with respect to the Mondragon system. Since many now seek solutions to economic and social problems in cooperativism, and see Mondragon as a prime example, such research is timely.

The Mondragon System of Worker Producer Cooperatives

The Mondragon system is offered as an outstanding example of workplace democracy in action (Oakeshott 1978; Thomas and Logan 1981; Johnson and Whyte 1982; Lindenfeld and Rothschild-Whitt 1982; Whyte 1982; Bradley and Gelb 1983; Gui 1984; Rothschild and Whitt 1986; Lindenfeld 1986). The system comprises over a hundred firms employing 19,000 worker-owners. They produce a variety of goods such as machine tools, stoves and refrigerators, electronic equipment, kitchen furniture, bicycles, and dairy and other agricultural products. Exports account for a quarter of goods produced. Additional Mondragon co-ops provide high-tech R&D, education, and health and social services. The Basque government now supports a series of Basque nursery schools begun by the Mondragon system.

Redundant workers return to school or work in other co-ops as needed. The highest paid director earns no more than three times the salary of the lowest-paid worker, in contrast to the average Basque firm ratio of 15 to 1, or the ratio in large U.S. corporations of over 100 to 1. Individual workers' private accounts receive 70 percent of the profit or surplus; the rest is allocated to community or co-op needs. The system is coordinated by its own cooperative bank, the Caja Laboral Popular, the most successful "people's bank" on record.

Some 28 percent of the system's workers are female. In addition, Auzo Lagun, a married women's cooperative, cooks and cleans for other cooperatives, and its craftswomen build the heavy industrial equipment needed for this work.

The 30-year Mondragon experience is more successful than any other large-scale worker-ownership venture. Compared, for example, with Yugoslavian labor-managed firms (Gui 1984), with the Japanese model (Bradley and Gelb 1983), and with private firms in Euskadi and Great Britain (Oakeshott 1978; Thomas and Logan 1981), Mondragon co-ops provide a greater degree of participation, accountability of management, more effective ways of defining property rights so as to minimize problems of investment, and greater efficiency, productivity, and creation of new jobs.

Mondragon's success is attributed to many factors: the special cultural characteristics of the Basques; the isolated mountain setting of this industrial community and the geographic stability of its residents; Franco's repression beginning in the 1930s, which encouraged people to try anything that worked; Spain's economic growth in the 1960s, during the co-ops' early years. Most, however, attribute a great deal of Mondragon's success to the presence of a strong and dedicated leader, the young priest Fr. Jose Maria Arizmendiarrieta, commonly shortened, as is the

Basque wont, to Arizmendi. He was an activist, with a vision of a better society based on Christian and socialist principles, toward which cooperativism would be a first step. The primary goal was to create employment.

Fr. Arizmendi's perception of women's place was largely hearth and home, but from the beginning women participated in the cooperative enterprise. Contradictory themes of economic equality for men and women permeate his work to such an extent, however, that some wonder if a woman actually wrote certain sections (Azurmendi 1984). He was a shrewd but practical man. A hard worker, he pushed others to their limits, but he also understood the situation and knew what would work at the time.

Fr. Arizmendi first supported co-op technical education for Mondragon's youth in the 1940s. He urged the community to support this effort, placing baskets for pledges on corner lamp posts. The community responded; the school was a success for the boys who entered. Graduates went elsewhere for their engineering degrees, then returned. The first co-op, Ulgor, was formed by 5 graduates in 1956, employing 24 men and 2 women. Their production of heating stoves flourished. Ulgor is now the largest of the cooperatives; it employs 3,000 workers and produces a variety of large appliances.

In 1958, Fr. Arizmendi strongly urged the new cooperative members to form their own people's bank. Private banks would be unlikely to provide the necessary capital for worker-owned firms. Members were skeptical, one recalled: "We told him yesterday we were craftsmen, foremen, and engineers. Today we are trying to learn how to be managers and executives. Tomorrow you want us to become bankers. That is impossible" (Johnson and Whyte 1982:180).

It was, of course, not impossible, and the Caja Laboral Popular, the working people' credit union, is today one of the most successful "people's banks" in history. A loophole in Spanish law allowed a fraction more interest to those who deposited their savings in such an institution. The thrifty community responded by shifting their money to the Caja. Co-ops are not unusual in Euskadi, accounting for some 10 to 15 percent of the economy. The strength of the Mondragon system lies in the Caja.

The Caja coordinates all aspects of the now nationwide system—research and development, planning, investment, and marketing. New co-op ventures apply to the Caja, which researches the market and judges the soundness of the proposed project. Proposers must have, or can borrow from the Caja, start-up cash. Each new member may also borrow the several thousand dollars necessary to obtain a job.

The cooperatives pay each worker-owner a salary. In addition, each co-op distributes 10 to 15 percent of its surplus or profit to the community for health, education, and other benefits. Another 15 to 20 percent goes to the co-op's reserve fund. The rest, 70 percent of profits, is distributed to members' own private capital accounts, according to their income; accounts receive at least 6 percent interest, double that in recent years. (This is a far cry from profit-sharing firms in the United States, which may set aside 5 percent of profits to "share.") Members must take 100 percent of this account plus interest at retirement, 80 percent if they leave earlier, 70 percent if they are fired. (There has been only one strike in the system's history. Years ago, Ulgor's governing body of workers fired a number of workers who struck over job classifications. This experience was attributed in part to the size of Ulgor. New co-ops are now set at no more than a few hundred.) If a firm operates at a loss, however, this must come from reserve funds, or workers' accounts.

The General Assembly of each cooperative comprises all members (workers) and elects—one person, one vote—a management board. This board appoints a manager and judge who is best fit for the job of overall coordinator. All other managers and supervisors are similarly appointed. The Assembly also elects a "watchdog" social council, which, although advisory only, joins the board to oversee management. The General Assembly also votes on investment patterns and other matters of import. Mondragon's wage structure is one of the outstanding features of the system. As noted previously, the pay ratio is not to exceed 3:1.

In the next chapter, I will use feminist criteria to evaluate the condition of women in the Mondragon Producer Cooperatives. The chapter is both descriptive of this co-op experience and critical of the missing feminist dimension. From a liberal perspective, I focus on similarities and differences between women and men at work within the cooperatives. I examine, from a socialist perspective, the problems of cooperative ventures set within a context of the market economy of monopoly capitalism. From a radical feminist perspective, I note the role of family, church, state, and military institutions. In Chapter 7, I explore relationships between these institutions and the organization and content of gender and technology. As the utopian left and feminists have done in the past, I will explore the erotic components of gender and cooperative relations, and, finally, the connections between eroticism and military institutions as opposed to cooperative influences on gender and technology.

Note

[1] Barbara Ilsey (1988), for example, documents the increase in women's mortality rates compared with men as an area in Southern India moved into the industrial age. This, she says, is the result of two complementary processes: women lost economic opportunity, while men gained more of the advantages of the system coming into being. This is an example of change, or modernization, *within* a patriarchal framework.

CHAPTER 6

Women Workers in the Mondragon System of Producer Cooperatives

Gender, technology, and military institutions are the subjects of the next chapter. Here, I discuss gender stratification in the Mondragon cooperatives, and relative power between men and women in the culture and the community.

Women's experiences at the workplace can be quite different from those of men, and these gender-based differences in power—gender stratification—affect workers and organizations (Acker and Van Houten 1974; Hacker 1979a; Kanter 1979). Feldberg and Glenn (1979) argue for a combination of "job" and "gender" models in the analysis of industry. More than a decade of research reveals the explanatory power added to theories of work when gender is considered. Indeed, we proceed at our peril when we do not consider gender (see Acker 1980; Chafetz 1984; Kahn-Hutt et al. 1982). One cannot understand women's condition at work in isolation from other institutions such as family (Acker 1982; Glazer 1984; Hartmann 1977; Huber and Spitze 1983; Sokoloff 1980; Stacey 1983), education (Hacker 1983a), military (Hacker and Hacker 1987; Enloe 1983), politics (Ferguson 1984; Hanawalt 1986; Kornegger 1975), or leisure (de Lauretis 1987; Peiss 1986). Scholarship increasingly focuses on women and development (Kandiyoti 1987; Papanek 1987), and on gender and the international division of labor (Ward 1984; Nash and Kelly 1983). While feminist literature needs more analyses of class, the literature on workplace democracy is somewhat retarded in analysis of gender (Feldberg 1981). Acker (1982) finds scholars and trade unionists alike locked in male-centered models of work and workers; women are perceived as peripheral. A single book reports contemporary women's experience in industrial cooperatives; Wajcman's (1983) poignant ethnography describes the failure of a British women's cooperative, poorly supported and operating within a hostile environment.

The Mondragon system of industrial cooperatives in the Basque Country of northern Spain is the most successful group of large-scale worker-owned and -managed cooperatives in industrial society. Cooperative structure can stimulate more democratic participation at work than traditional organizations. As I suggested in Chapter 5, however, democracy and participation in the larger society affect this workplace goal for both men and women. The present chapter examines these phenomena from several perspectives.

For seven months, I lived and worked in Euskadi (the Basque name for Basque Country), in the city of Donostia (San Sebastian), 30 miles from Mondragon, where the now nationwide system originated and is still headquartered. The Basque name of the city is Arrasate, but the system uses the Spanish, Mondragon. This city of some 30,000 is near to Donostia, but the rugged mountain road takes an hour or more to drive. There are no trains; all materials and goods come and go by truck. Mondragon is neither rural nor rustic. It is a modern industrial city. One comes upon it, as most Basque cities, suddenly—there are no outskirts. On the right, then the left, stand rows of buildings two or three stories high, 8 to 20 flats each. Newer housing terraces up the side of the mountain, artfully designed and landscaped, still built in multiflat clusters. In the center of the city stand a handful of highrises. I saw only one freestanding house in the city; it appeared to have been converted to public purpose. Population in Euskadi ranks among the densest in Europe. "They say that's what makes us so 'crispy,'" a resident said. "We live so close together."

I interviewed co-op and non-co-op members in management, education, research, and service work. I stayed and played with production workers in the city of Mondragon on several weekends. I gathered systematic data on jobs and pay from two selected co-ops, and from two comparable Basque private firms. This is what I found.

As described in Chapter 5, one can take a loan or purchase direct a position as a member-worker. Prospective members undergo a period of education and probation, chiefly to show whether or not their values are truly cooperative. Allocation or selection of work seems quite traditionally gendered. There seems to be more resistance to traditional, gendered placement among women technicians and managers than among production workers; production workers show more resistance to hierarchy and control.

To assess the degree to which the Mondragon cooperatives provide opportunities for women, I looked at employment, position, and pay, much as we did in the study of AT&T (see Chapter 2). Few systematic data exist for employment comparing men and women in the cooperatives, but with the exception of a bicycle production co-op, what data existed were freely given. Such data had to be gathered through interviews with each co-op director. Although on the cutting edge of Spain's computer industry and forecasting, the Caja keeps no overall comparisons of employment by gender and occupational level. (It took the federal government, however, to obtain such data from corporations in the United States.)

Ulgor is the oldest and the largest of the cooperatives. In 1976, one-fifth of its 2,000 workers were women (Thomas and Logan 1981). Some 86 percent of the women, but only 37 percent of the men, were employed under level 1.5 (of the 3:1 pay levels; see Chapter 5). In contrast, 10 percent of the men, but less than 1 percent of women, held jobs above level 2.00. Only one woman has ever directed one of these larger, older, manufacturing co-ops.

The situation is similar at Fagorelectronica, a co-op that manufactures electronic components for TV channel selectors, automobiles, kitchen appliances, and the like. Of 580 workers, 70 percent are women; 96 percent are employed below level 1.5, compared to 56 percent of the men; 20 percent of the men, but only 1 percent of the women, work above level 2.00. In recent years, there has been some increase in women managers and in the number of women on the board of directors. Two women have joined the board since 1980. There has been an increase of one percentage point in females at upper-level jobs during the past five years.

I toured Fagorelectronica, though it was not easy. Although I thought arrangements had been made, the front office said no when I arrived; it was "impossible today." But I had met a worker the day before, who had, on her own invited me to see the plant. I asked for her, and the tour was approved. By and large, the physical layout of work and the equipment were not dissimilar from electronics plants I have toured in the United States. The plant was large, airy, and light, however, and the people were more relaxed. In the first room, middle-aged male craftsmen, classified at level 1.8, repaired equipment. In the next, twenty or so women and four men (level 1.23) assembled diodes, inserting wires into preformed plastic parts. Parts moved along conveyers to stations where two or three worked together. I asked about robotics. My guide, Rosa, a higher-level (2.2) technical worker, said perhaps robotics would be introduced in the future, but at present labor was cheaper. And some processes, related to baking on the insulation, for example, might be more dangerous with automatic rather than human operation.

I asked about potential health hazards from the baking process. Specialists had come the week before from Lagun Aro, the social services co-op, to take air samples, and all was well. I told her a story from *Science for the People*, the magazine of the Science Resource Center in Cambridge, Massachusetts: The Spanish government had failed to release the brand names of wines found to contain harmful additives; after its own research, Mondragon published the names of the brands, an act the Spanish government reportedly called another example of "Basque informational terrorism." She smiled.

Two women operated large machinery, the blades of which rose and fell, clipping wires and trimming diode edges. A man operated machinery stamping voltage on the diodes, then packaged them in plastic coils for shipping. Two more rooms, more diode assembly. At the final stage, inspection, a female supervisor with some spare time filled in, replacing unmarked diodes with those properly stamped.

Quality control was next. It was quieter, employing about half women and men. Testers (levels 1.3 or 1.35) operated oscilloscopes. "That man in the white coat?" I asked. "A boss of six or seven women; his level is 1.9," was the reply. The manager of quality control was a 2.3 or 2.4, the same level as the woman engineer who was my guide's temporary boss. Her permanent supervisor was a male at level 2.7. The general manager of the co-op was classified at level 2.8. A bulletin board sported announcements of various social events, largely athletic, including one women's football (soccer) team.

Clara, with whom I stayed in Mondragon, is a young production worker at this plant. She lives alone and owns a large and handsome three-bedroom flat in the new subdivisions built up the side of the mountain: large windows, balcony, blond wood floors and paneling, Scandinavian art and women's posters on the walls. I asked what her friends and family thought of her political activism. "Oh, they may not agree, but they know me." Relations are congenial. Her off-hours are a round of political meetings, study, and writing. On the evening paseo, the round of bars and streets, she exchanged greetings with almost everyone. "You know everybody," I said. "Yes, but I talk only with some." Conversation appears to display alliance. A young worker at another plant had described an overbearing supervisor, and I had asked what she did about it. "I don't talk to him," she told me.

At dinner with a number of women co-op and non-co-op workers, I learned all had been born and raised in Mondragon. I asked if they ever wanted to move, to Donostia, perhaps. "Maybe," said one. "But my parents are here. How would I get a job in another city?" We discussed the different patterns of mobility in the United States, where people move an average of 13 times during their lives, and hiring is more likely based on credentials. They decided the high geographic mobility had both positive and negative aspects. One would learn more by moving round, but would lose ties of community, trust, and solidarity.

Members at the Fagorelectronica plant work three shifts. Care for children over a year old may be provided by nurseries, community women, or in some instances husbands on different shifts. Parental leave for childbirth is more likely than any other leave to preserve one's position. Although such leave is available to both sexes, it is taken only by women. Marriage affects men and women differently. Men at the upper levels are more likely than men at the lower levels to be married. For women, the reverse is true.

In Auzo Lagun, the married women's co-op, 317 women, average age 47, provide hot meals (average level 1.40), cleaning (average level 1.35), and other services for co-ops in or near Mondragon. A group of 24 craftswomen (average level 1.40) construct the heavy industrial equipment needed for this work. The brochure for Auzo Lagun displays photos of women in all but these craft jobs. The average level for the women providing administrative services for Auzo Lagun is 2.00. The sole male is director. The co-op was formed in 1969, in defiance of Spanish law, which barred married women from working at most occupations in private firms until 1970, and in cooperatives until 1973. Women work four-hour shifts to avoid taking time away from family. Initially, Basque men resisted. Many men and women felt that married women belonged at home. These attitudes changed as the extra money helped pay for a car, for a better flat, or to make ends meet.

I asked Asun, the personnel director, how levels were set for each job. A committee of representatives elected by the workers makes a yearly evaluation. And, yes, there is much wrangling and heated debate at these times, but once decisions are made, people go along with them.

Home and family remain women's responsibility. The biggest problem at Auzo Lagun is absenteeism—when a child or a husband or the worker herself is ill, she misses work. Men as a rule do not stay at home when someone else is sick. One complaint is that although the women work half-time, they pay the full-time rate for cooperative benefits. The women enjoy cooperative work more than staying at home or working for a private firm. They cite the greater degree of freedom and autonomy on the job, and the sociability and feeling of community. Even progressive critics of the system had only words of praise for this cooperative ("Those are great women over there.").

One cannot compare the sitution of women in Auzo Lagun or the larger co-ops with that of workers in private Basque firms, because nothing comparable exists. Basque firms are small relative to the large co-ops. I selected two co-ops with comparable firms in the private economy. After consulting with a director of a Caja branch in Donostia, and with printouts on Basque firms by industry and size, I selected Danona, a printing and publishing co-op, and Leniz, a kitchen furniture manufacturing co-op. Both had enough workers for fine analysis, and relatively comparable private firms nearby, Valverde and Vega.

Employment

Overall, one might expect much less employment opportunity for women in the cooperatives than in Basque industry, given that the co-ops' industrial mix is shaded toward heavy industry rather than small shops, services, or textiles, traditional fields for women workers. The difference in women's percentage of employment between the co-ops (28 percent) and Basque country in general (25 percent), however, reflects a slightly greater opportunity for women in the co-ops. Data in Table 6.1 also show, for this limited comparison, that although men have greater employment

Table 6.1 Comparison of Employment,
Co-op vs Private, Percentage Female

Printing		
Danona co-op	20	(N = 52)
Valverde	22	(N = 91)
Furniture manufacturing		
Leniz co-op	25	(N = 117)
Vega	09	(N = 206)

[1] *Source:* Data from personnel directors of each firm.

opportunity in both co-ops and private firms, women's employment rates in co-ops are similar to or much higher than in the private firms.

Location in the Occupational Structure

In both printing firms, lowest-level workers are male helpers or handymen, followed by all-women crews who work in the bindery, inserting material by hand (Table 6.2). Only in the co-op do these women earn more than the male helpers. The atmosphere in the co-op seemed remarkably more relaxed than in the private firms, particularly regarding interaction among women workers and between women workers and their supervisors. In the co-op, women in hand-bindery chatted, looked up, and moved about freely. In the private firm, hand-binders stood working silently, casting only sidelong glances.

In printing, then, most women work as binders, with some in administrative services, as clerical workers or assistants. Men so employed tend to perform similar tasks, but at higher rank and pay. A few women work in photoreproduction or composition. All pressmen, other craft workers, and management in both firms are male. The private firm tends more than the co-op to provide women with clerical rather than production jobs.

In the kitchen furniture firms, too, women work in lowest-level all-female assembly work, and in clerical or administrative assistant positions, with again more clerical than production work for women in the private firm. With the exception of two women in the private firm, skilled craft and all upper-level office and managerial jobs are held by men.

In the co-op, my female guide from the front office stopped to talk often with asemblers and finishers. Occasionally they would show me with pride an especially nice piece of work. In the private firm, despite several requests, we somehow never made it to the area where the four female production workers performed their tasks.

Table 6.2 Distribution of Men and Women over
Occupational Structure: Co-op vs Private Firm (in percentages)

	Co-op		Private	
	Male	Female	Male	Female
Printing				
Unskilled and semiskilled				
handymen, helpers, movers, storage, etc.	14	0	12	0
hand-binders	0	70	0	53
cutters, staplers, etc.	21	0	6	0
Skilled				
drafting, makeup, photoreprod., press workers, etc.	48	10	65	10
Administrative assistants, sales, other commercial/clerical	7	20	8	37
Management	10	0	8	0
Totals	100	100	99	100
N =	42	10	72	19
Furniture manufacturing				
Unskilled				
bag fillers	—	—	0	14
final assembly	0	79	—	—
Semiskilled[a]				
Forklift operators, loaders, sanders, etc.	50	0	8	4
Lower and middle clerical/office	0	21	10	77
Skilled[b]	15	0	70	4
Highly skilled and			4	0
upper office/management[c]	35	0	8	0
Totals	100	100	100	99
N =	88	29	184	22

[1] *Source:* Data from personnel directors, interviews, observation.

[a] Includes lower-seniority skilled workers, at private firm.

[b] Includes semiskilled at higher seniority levels, private firm.

[c] Highly skilled and management are grouped in the highest of three categories for which data were provided by the co-op. This is sufficient for our purposes, given that there are no women workers at or above this level.

Pay

Cooperatives do not succeed by paying lower wages or selling at lower prices. Superior productivity is the basis for survival, not an underpaid work force. Thus, a co-op's average wage is set to match that of surrounding industry. Within each cooperative, the 3:1 pay ratio means that managers and professional people will earn less than their counterparts in private industry; lower-level workers will earn more. Since women are more often found at the lower levels, their earning capacity should be greater in co-ops than in private industry. Table 6.3 indicates that for representative jobs, women and other low-waged people (and, in fact, all the selected workers at the printing co-op) receive higher wages in co-ops than in private firms. This was true for clerical workers, perhaps, in only one of the two comparisons.

In summary, women in co-ops clearly face barriers to equal

Table 6.3 Wages for Selected Occupations in Basque Cooperatives and Private Firms

| | Printing | | Furniture Manufacturing | |
	Cooperative	Private firm	Cooperative	Private firm
Unskilled (bindery, assembly)	$ 3.05	$1.99	$3.18	$2.51
Skilled (e.g., photoreproduction, carpentry)	3.39	2.79	3.90	3.97
(e.g., makeup, mechanicals)	3.62	2.98	4.64	4.79
Clerical/administrative assistant	3.62	2.98	3.66	4.29
Management	11.30[a]	5.98	7.32	8.73

Source: All data from personnel directors.
[a] This salary is one of the "temporary exceptions"; the manager was at 5:1 rather than 3:1 because of the difficulty of recruiting a manager at the cooperative's standard wage.

opportunity similar to those in all industrial societies. But compared to private firms, cooperativism can be advantageous to women and other lower-earning workers. On two of the three traditional measures of employment equality—employment and pay—women fare better in co-ops than in private firms. In addition, benefits are better (Oakeshott 1982), and the healthy share of profits owned by each worker, accumulating interest, adds up to considerably better lifetime savings at retirement. In terms of *kind* of work, the structure of the private firms appears to provide women with greater opportunity for clerical than production work, and perhaps some greater opportunity to break into traditional male crafts.

Approaching the problem from this liberal economic viewpoint, however, does not challenge the occupational structure as given; it merely argues for equal opportunity within it. Nor does it question the ownership or distribution of profits produced by the workers, or modes of control. It lacks historical perspective on the ebb and flow of men and women into and out of various occupations, especially during periods of technological change, and the reasons for these shifts. For insights relevant to women on these issues, we need a different perspective.

We must recognize that "management," in the analytic categories above, leaves out the top level in the private firm—the capitalists. Neither of the two private firm personnel directors I interviewed could guess at an income or asset figure for the wealthy families who owned the controlling interests in these firms. The co-ops, on the other hand, are coordinated by the Caja, whose highest-paid worker should earn no more than $10.26 (3:1) to $17.10 per hour (5:1; see Table 6.3, note a), or $2,962 per month. No wealthy capitalists at the top receive the worker-produced profit; rather this is reinvested in the co-op and in the community, and held in savings for the worker-members.

Although a co-op job may never be lost, some women production workers did complain about being sent home during slack time more readily than male craft workers, who sometimes appeared to be doing make-work. For married women, the economic effects of this downtime are not considered so serious. The family is the basic economic unit. For women who are single and want to stay that way, or perhaps to marry late, the implications are more severe.

Still, there is less incentive to automate lower-level work in the co-ops, since other work must be found for the displaced. In private firms, many production-level jobs have been automated, or the work has been passed on to the consumer. The furniture manufacturer does no final assembly, employing only the four women who fill plastic bags with screws. These practices explain in part why private firms have a higher proportion than co-ops of women in clerical rather than production jobs—the capitalist firms have eliminated many production jobs.

In capitalist societies, taxpayers and the unemployed largely pay the costs of automation (Noble 1984); owners take the profits. Similarly, at the Basque capitalist plants, no one knew where or if the workers displaced over the years by automation were employed. Co-ops provide alternative work or education rather than unemployment. At Danona, six men will be replaced by a new four-color press. One is being retained for management. As for the others, I was told, "We will discuss and see." In another co-op, everyone worked one less hour each day to preserve employment for all. The cooperatives have created an alternative in which the largest share of profits belongs to workers as their private property, and in which both the costs and the benefits of automation are shared by all system members.

A socialist economist in Mondragon, Antxon Mendizabel, agrees that co-ops are more productive: no class struggle, no union, no strikes. Workers are management. Co-ops are much more flexible than capitalist firms: workers can agree to more or fewer hours, salaries can be adjusted up or down, labor can be moved from one site to another when needed. Investments are more productively planned and executed. Profits (surpluses) are higher, and the system is economically more dynamic than others. Finally, cooperativism is a good selling point to the Third World—"Ah, a worker-owned industrial co-op!" Last year, in fact, the People's Republic of China purchased an entire factory system from Mondragon.

Mendizabal notes, however, that a cooperative system

operating in a capitalist context will be inherently flawed. Since the co-ops must compete with capitalist firms, they must produce goods as determined by the market, organize work similarly, and spend no more on ecological concerns than the capitalist firms. Further, during periods of crisis one may be more secure in a co-op, but one cannot afford to think about others who are not members.

Mendizabel, like co-op management, foretells hard times ahead given the world economic crisis and competition from the cheaper, more oppressed laborers of Hong Kong, Korea, and Brazil. If the surrounding society is democratically organized, the co-op system will be beneficial, since its own structure is inherently egalitarian and mutual. But if society is not democratic, cooperatives will continue, in practice, to operate contrary to democratic principle in many ways.

Women face additional problems in a cooperative economy. Wages are set by the market, and the market is not sex blind. Women's work has been traditionally devalued, and women have faced more obstacles forcing a fair return for their work than men. Each co-op has its own 3:1 pay ratio. Thus, those holding jobs in co-ops characterized by traditionally male work will receive higher pay than those performing traditionally female work (see Table 6.4).

These differences are not great compared to the inequity in male and female earnings in the United States, or between primary and secondary labor markets, but even $.70 per hour over a working life can add up to a difference of tens of thousands of dollars (plus interest) at retirement for people doing similar work.

Table 6.4 Starting Wage at Selected Cooperatives (per hour)

Caja (bank) & Ikerlan (R&D)	$3.42
Ularco (manufacturing)	3.34
Leniz (furniture manufacturing)	3.18
Danona (printing)	3.05
Auzo Lagun (cooking, cleaning)	2.74

Contracting out for cheaper labor is often the first step toward the demise of cooperativism. The California garbage co-ops, for example, began to hire black workers at lower levels. These workers did not have access to co-op membership or benefits (Russell 1982). Literature on Mondragon, and my interviews, mentioned limited contracting for scarce skills, such as computer science. Unmentioned is the extensive contracting of women at lower levels. If a co-op is not served by Azo Lagun, non-co-op women are contracted from the private sector, at lower pay, to perform janitorial services. These workers are not included in the published 3:1 pay ratio, nor do they receive co-op benefits. There are other examples as well. A woman in Donostia had worked as a contract laborer for Mondragon's Fagor plant in Madrid. She and others visited houses, cleaning and inspecting components of kitchen appliances produced by Fagor. Earlier, this work had been performed by male co-op members' wives, who had benefits through their husbands' employment. As their numbers increased, single women began pressing for co-op membership and its benefits; they lost their jobs for this effort.

Competing with private firms and facing the same crises, the cooperatives do not want to take on new members in these temporary positions if alternatives can be found. Contracting cheaper female labor is one such alternative. This alternative is facilitated by women's economic dependence on the family wage and benefit practice (if not policy) of the cooperatives.

Feminist activists criticize several institutions—the Catholic church, the indifference of the system, sexism among Basque men—all of which tend to favor the traditional family. Those with a Marxist orientation acknowledge that theory and practice seldom challenge the structure of the family, the economic basis of the cooperatives. Women in the family take up the slack, absorbing costs otherwise borne by the co-ops. The socialist critique of cooperatives has yet to address these pressing problems of patriarchal institutions. Feminist critiques place matters in a more comprehensive framework, as in Judith Stacey's (1983) work on patriarchy and social revolution in China, described in Chapter 2. Such analyses are useful also for our study of the Mondragon cooperatives.

Elizabeth Croll's (1982) data from a production brigade of a people's commune in China showed that 68 percent of the women, compared to 40 percent of the men, clustered at jobs given low-wage grades, while at the highest grades, 2 percent were women and 23 percent were men. In each case, it is primarily women's responsibility for home and children that supposedly excludes them from equal roles in participatory workplace or community democracy. Despite China's socialist revolution, many patrilineal and patrilocal structures were retained, the family remained the basic economic unit, and traditional women's skills were devalued. Support for one's family, skill training, and solidarity were available primarily to men through participation in the Red Army (Stacey 1983). In the Israeli kibbutz, women's increasing responsibility for child care eventually precluded participation in more prestigious work, in the military, and in local committees and organizations of political significance (Blumberg 1976).

Socialist, rather than communist, solutions to the problem of distribution affected women in the Soviet Union, Cuba, and China. Rather than distributing goods and services according to need, which would address the economic problem of individual responsibility for child rearing, policies led to distribution according to work, or according to one's wage (Nazzari 1983). Even when societies mandate men and women equal responsibility for child care, or argue for the socialization of child care, these policies are seldom implemented. As Nazzari shows for Cuba, these measures demand resources and labor and compete with other national goals, especially military, and so policies favorable to women seldom prevail.

Thus for true workplace democracy, for a solution to the problem of gendered spheres, a communist economic solution to distribution—to each according to need—seems necessary. But this solution does not fully address the problem of control. A second possibility, then, is to incorporate antihierarchical, decentralized, anarchafeminist principles into workplace cooperative structure and process

(Ferguson 1984; Kornegger 1975). Such an approach requires sharing and demystifying the technical skills and knowledge of technocratic administration and transforming it into truly democratic structures of coordination. These goals, of course, are for the long term. A short-term solution—greater participation of women in technical and engineering fields—is necessary, but not sufficient, because as these fields undergo degradation, women and minorities are often encouraged into routinized sectors (Hacker 1983a).

Some argue that the Mondragon system operates so effectively because it is rooted in Basque culture, which is very solidary and egalitarian. If this is true, the experience could not be transplanted successfully to more individualistic cultures. But Basques themselves ask: If the culture alone is responsible, why Mondragon? Why not Bilbao or elsewhere in Euskadi? Their argument supports the potential for cooperatives in other cultures. In his presidential address before the American Sociological Association, William Foote Whyte (1982) challenged social scientists to study this social innovation, to learn what we can from these democratic structures. Given this debate, I report here some of my observations of Basque culture, including those relevant to gender stratification in that society.

Basque Culture and Society

Basque scholars trace their culture to prehistoric roots. Archaeological and historical evidence suggests that Basque-speaking peoples occupied their present homeland before the first Indo-European incursions (Bilbao 1985). The culture has, in any event, survived many centuries of war, invasion, and oppression, most recently under the Franco dictatorship of Spain. Basque Country, Euskadi, now comprises several territories spanning the formidable Pyrenees bounding France and Spain. In the northern part, nominally claimed by France, the economic base is pastoral/agricultural. In the southern part, claimed by Spain, it is industrial. Basques have mined and forged in these iron-rich mountains for hundreds of years.

Since Franco's death more than a decade ago, and especially after the recent election of a socialist government in Spain, Basques have won a state of semiautonomy. In 1980, three of the four southern territories achieved their own local, state, and federal government, the Comunidad Autonoma Vasca, still subject in many areas to Spanish law.

Institutions do not change overnight, and the legacy of the Franco regime persists, for instance, in the presence of the Civil Guard and the national police. This presence is disturbing, even to a visitor. I felt a sudden rage, for example, when I entered the post office and encountered a member of the Guard languidly holding his weapon and his gaze in my direction.

Basques are sharply divided on the issue of armed or nonviolent resistance. Only one of the five major parties, Herri Batasuna, refuses to denounce the armed and illegal counterforce, ETA (*Euzkadi ta Azkatasuna*, Basque Land and Liberty; see Payne 1975:242–245). Amnesty for political exiles gains more public support. When a member of ETA is arrested, "disappeared," or killed, reaction is divided. But on occasion, as during my stay, the Guard blunders. A young Basque man, relatively apolitical, from a modest and respected family in a small village, was arrested and disappeared. Demonstrations and demands continued until his body was located. Spanish authorities would not allow his physician and one from Amnesty International to attend the autopsy. The ensuing general strike cleared streets and shops alike. Nothing and no one worked, and an eerie silence replaced the usual intensity of everyday life.

Mondragon is generally considered among the more political of Basque towns and areas, strong in its resistance to Franco during the civil war. But my attempts to locate the cooperatives in one or another of the left ideologies or parties—particularly social anarchist, given its structure—consistently met the response, "That's politics. We are only interested in creating jobs." In this way, perhaps, the cooperative effort is buffered against the cross-currents of Basque political life.

In contrast to the United States, Basque culture seemed to me incredibly solidary and egalitarian. The culture holds in tension elements of individualism and collectivity, a tension barely felt in the United States. Antihierarchical values and behavior seem evident in every daily interaction—on buses, in offices, in bars, and on the streets. There is little evidence of class background or social status in dress or demeanor. People dress casually and speak up and out most freely. No one seeks advantage over another without hearing about it. Mental and manual work are equally valued. Status comes from being Basque.

Social life takes place in groups. Children grow up in cuadrillas, play groups based on cross-status residential patterns, where playmates come from all walks of life. The anthropological literature mentions all-male groups, especially the gastronomical societies, but social groups are also all-female and mixed. Friendships are lifelong, and, some say, stronger than family bonds. Basque schoolchildren are more likely than those in other industrial countries to prefer a cooperative pay structure to one wherein a few can earn a lot, but the many earn much less (Johnson and Whyte 1982). A study of a Basque village and its farm-to-city migration, underscores the primacy of other nonmarket motivation. Greenwood (1976) argues that for Basques, and perhaps others as well, the meaning of life, and of dignity in work, may account for more than do economic factors.

Familiar American patterns of extreme individualism at play or work seem virtually absent in Basque culture. I asked one women what kinds of leisure activity she liked. She told me she enjoyed going to the mountain with friends (a favorite weekend activity for most), biking with friends, talking in the bars with friends. I asked what would happen if she wanted to go to a park. "I would go with my friends who wanted to go," she responded. And what if she wanted to be alone, perhaps to think, or read a book under a tree? Puzzled, she answered, "Oh, well, people would *look*, you know, give you the *look*." Not in hostility, but from curiosity or worry over what might be wrong. Very solidary, very collective. Did she have to go away for her college education? "Yes! Thirty miles!" I also asked her, a management-level worker in one of the major co-ops, about her plans for the future. I said that in the United States such

112

a person with that kind of education and experience might be looking for the next rung up the ladder, or a better position somewhere else. Her response: "Me? Move to Barcelona?! To Madrid?! Pah!" she spit. "With whom would I drink?!"

Social life is intense; one is seldom alone. An intricate and elaborate network of communication operates in the streets and bars of each village and city. It is in the streets and bars, not the homes, where sociability takes place. Reports show there are more bars in Gipuzkoa province, where Donostia and Mondragon are located, than in the whole of the European Common Market. (There were 25 on my block alone.) Many are as well-lit as a friend's kitchen and have a similar atmosphere. Their main purpose is social rather than sexual or alcoholic. In ritual form, groups roam the streets, walk from bar to bar, taking a coffee or a small glass in each, chatting, laughing, arguing, passing news, doing business. In Mondragon, we were joined one night by a visiting feminist from Holland. She joked about the evening ritual: "I order a drink, sit down, ready to get into deep conversation, when somebody yells 'Vamos!' Time to go!"

Zubillaga (1987) cites the importance of the streets, as well as media and institutions, for the intense political dialogue that forms a basic part of Basque life. Once I said it would be impossible to organize a demonstration overnight. Who would do all the calling, the organizing? And only about half the homes have telephones, anyway. My comments were simply ignored. A faster form of communication is the bars. The demonstration was attended by thousands. In my view, these networks and conditions of solidarity and equality do support cooperativism and industrial democracy. But there is no reason we cannot learn from the forms of social life as well as from those of the industrial cooperatives.

The struggles for Basque autonomy within the Spanish state and independence within a federation of European cultures are central political issues for many Basque parties, and are important for women's organizations as well. One politically radical women's group in Donostia dealt with a range of issues while I was there: a predominantly female work force at a shoelace factory facing closure; a woman injured by the attack of a man she rejected in a bar; workshops on violence, lesbianism, and health care. Their letter to the more political Basque newspaper, *Egin*, announced: "The Rapists Have Names," and provided these, along with addresses. But primary energy that year turned toward feminist participation in demonstrations against the Spanish government, particularly the reversal of policy, and its new decision to maintain NATO ties with the United States.

An all-women demonstration drew trains carrying thousands to the village of Eibar, where a privately owned factory produced military helicopters. Women covered its entrance with the "web of life," woven in colored strands of yarn. Songs were lively and plentiful; speeches were few, spontaneous, and brief.

There is an expression, "The Basques have no fear." This demeanor, in my experience, characterizes women as well as men. I saw elderly women as well as men marching, in part sympathetically, in part to protect the young, at demonstrations considered vulnerable to official violence. And at the women's demonstration in Eibar, when my Spanish was still rudimentary, I learned we were shouting at the heavily armed and ever-present Civil Guard that they were full of shit.

The Iberian Peninsula's women's movement—Spanish, Basque, and others—celebrated its tenth year in 1985. In Barcelona, an abortion was videotaped and shown. The authorities acted quickly to find the guilty, uncredentialed women responsible. All 4,000 women in attendance claimed the honors. The March 8, 1986, celebration in Donostia emphasized health and culture through film, art, crafts, and lectures on sexuality and reproduction. A lecture on lesbianism was attended by 100 women. The International Women's Day dinner drew 200. In the much smaller city of Mondragon, 100 women ate, drank champagne, and danced until 2:00 a.m.

In many ways, Basque culture seemed to me among the least gender-differentiated of modern societies, in appearance, style, and presentation of self. When I asked how the Spanish differed from the Basques, often the reply was a mimicry of exaggerated gender differences in speech and movement assumed among the Spanish in the south. A Spanish man, in turn, imitated the lower, throaty speech and lack of coyness among Basque women. The question itself may elicit only such stereotypes, but Basque men and women alike value strength. Basque women appeared to me both more and less independent than women in the United States. Everyday relations between Basque men and women were more trusting and mutual, but also more reserved.

I thought it possible that sexuality was muted, but pervasive, not so individually or genitally focused as in the United States, certainly not as fascinated with power and powerlessness. As Talmon's (1972) study of the kibbutz suggests, collective life in childhood can establish open, warm, but deeroticized relations between boys and girls, given the lack of opportunity for a private, possessive relationship. In one group of young people, for example, a close friendship between an American student and his Basque male friend led to temporary ostracism by the friend's group. In another case, a young American student accepted an invitation to a Sting concert, to find her date arrived with three of his friends.

Some data to indicate a more relaxed attitude toward sexuality among the Basques. A three-generation study of Basque women in cities, in fishing villages, and in rural villages showed that over half favored premarital sex and viewed masturbation positively; a third to a half thought homosexuality an acceptable form of expression for those who chose (del Valle et al. 1985). Euskadi was in fact among the last of European countries to be Christianized.

But many feminists with whom I spoke disagreed. In another study, del Valle (1983) sensitively analyses the restrictive use of space accorded to women in the family, in the streets and public life, and in myths. This is reinforced through movements in various ritual forms of dance and festival. Women's groups are encircled and sometimes threatened, perhaps reflecting a fear of women's power. Another report has it that Basque women place sexual relations sixth on a list of priorities for a good relationship, and that Basque men prefer a good dinner. Some young university women described sexual relations as "very repressed." "Because of all the priests and the nuns," according to a law student. A social worker spoke of a high degree of frigidity among Basque women. I asked what that meant. "Well, the men grab at them and want sex in a hurry, and they don't like that," she responded.

There is relative silence among young girls on the theme of sexuality. This silence in the home, and emphasis on virtue, is coupled with an exaltation of virginity before marriage. The goal is to prevent pregnancy (del Valle et al. 1985). Women seem to deal with sexuality and eroticism much as we do in the United States, although again with more reserve and less bawdiness than has been my experience to witness in working-class culture. For all but a few, sexuality is a topic of conversation after the meeting, over dinner or coffee, when the men are gone. In the women's movement, however, sexuality is the subject of vigorous discussion.

Anthropological literature is ambiguous on the role of women in Euskadi. Basque culture is described as notably patriarchal, but women also emerge as strong, independent, sometimes "matriarchal," equal to men in every respect. Until recently, this literature was unaffected by the feminist transformation of knowledge in the field (Stacey and Thorne 1986). Now, Basque women's studies scholars question this mythic strength of women. Research such as that directed by Teresa del Valle at the Seminar on Woman, University of the Basque Country, indicates that however democratic the culture may appear, people expect work will be central for men, and the private sphere of hearth and home central for women.

Indeed, few married women work for pay. In *Mujer vasca: Imagen y realidad* (del Valle et al. 1985), feminist anthropologists explore the life of women, not only in rural and fishing villages, but also in the urban centers that most characterize modern Basque culture in Spain. The dominant roles for women are wife and, especially, mother—strong, hardworking, nurturant, and clean. The implications of the word "clean" are both moral and physical; everywhere, home and workplace, cleaning is women's work. Men are valued as good workers. *Indarra* (inner strength) is associated with men in their public activities; with women, only in childbirth and the family. *Adur* (mystic and mysterious power), both good and evil, is associated only with women. Women's strength is to be directed toward husband and family. Even in radical politics, women are expected to support their men in the revolution.

Of Euskadi's college graduates, 39 percent are female, with highest concentrations in traditional fields of education and health. Single women's labor force participation equals that of men, but less than 10 percent of married women work. These figures are similar to those for the rest of Spain (Gobierno Vasco 1983). Unemployment is somewhat higher now in the industrial areas of the north than in Spain as a whole, but in both, these figures hover around 30 percent. Women's rates are slightly higher than those of men, and the family must absorb the unemployed.

The traditional family is quite strong in this Catholic country, and the Catholic church is quite powerful in education. I asked a Jesuit priest, a college president and specialist on Mondragon, how the co-ops planned for future needs of the family, as women's employment would surely increase. His answer was rather abrupt: "The co-ops have nothing to do with the family." But women, especially younger women, search for alternatives to economic dependence on husbands' wages. As more women live independent of the family, violence against them is on the increase, according to feminist groups.

However egalitarian the roots of Basque culture, patriarchal modernization and the Catholic church, among other forces, help direct men to the public sphere, women to the private. Organized sports and the military are also important factors in gender and segregation. Although the Basques have their own tradition of relations between military and education, mentioned in the next chapter, there is now no Basque army. All young men, however, must serve in the Spanish army. During my stay, two groups on my block suffered disruption as some of the young men were taken away. In

117

Chapter 4, I suggested that modernization is deeply rooted in patriarchal military institutions. This continues to affect concepts of gender, technology, and work in Euskadi as well as elsewhere, but here the most direct military influence comes from the occupying state of Spain.

Zubillaga (1987) notes that Spanish militarization affects Euskadi women, as militarization affects women everywhere, through distortion of budgets and a shift toward male-centered high-tech industrial organization, with accompanying automation and layoffs. Militarization, she says, with its centralized and hierarchical forms, reinforces traditional male values of hierarchy, honor, and discipline. It strengthens the forces limiting women's roles to mother and wife, within the family. Iberian feminists resist this military influence, local, national, or international.

These, then, are some impressions of contradictory strains held in tension in Basque culture, relevant to gender and power in the private and public spheres, and explored more generally in Chapter 7.

The Mondragon cooperative structure benefits women workers in many ways, but, as elsewhere, several factors continue to structure inequality based on gender: market-set wages, contract labor of lower-waged women, unpaid domestic labor, and women's economic dependence on the husband's salary and benefits (see Benenson 1984). An additional problem is increasing reliance on professional expertise, as the system modernizes its technological core. Professionalism entails control over specialized knowledge, an important obstacle to democratic participation in co-operatives where production is based on complex technology (Rothschild and Whitt 1986). This control diminishes autonomy and participation of workers at lower levels, where women predominate.

In the next chapter I report concerns voiced by women workers with whom I spoke—concerns for autonomy at work and economic independence from the family at home. I link these issues to technological change guided by material and ideological interests historically rooted in patriarchal military institutions. These interests are embedded in part in Spanish tradition and to a lesser extent in the history of Basque science, technology, and society itself.They are, however, also imported to Euskadi through models of European professional education, and may find current expression in new, technocratic forms of administration. These tendencies are contradicted by egalitarian elements of Basque culture, by the democratic structure of the cooperative workplace and the Polytecnica, and by the collective activities of Basque women in feminist and political groups.

CHAPTER 7

Gender and Technology in the Mondragon System

The cooperative can be an oppositional form to current patterns of power and authority at work. The Mondragon system, compared with others and with the traditional workplace, is on many counts astounding, vibrant, effective. But a more helpful comparison is with a potential feminist and cooperative workplace, where women and men work together with participatory technologies, technologies that have a gentler touch with people and the environment. Feminism can counter antidemocratic influences embedded in part in new technologies and administrative practices.

Mondragon is known as a system of democratically structured producer cooperatives, yet the condition of women workers there is only somewhat better, relative to men, than in capitalist or already-existing socialist organizations. There are three major obstacles to gender equality in the Mondragon system. First, waged or not, women have responsibility for the home. The collective response to child care and care of other dependents has not been sufficiently supported by the cooperatives (Barrett and McIntosh 1982). This is not characteristic of Basque society alone, but of all industrial societies (see Nazzari 1983). Second, a capitalist market devalues collective social goals, as noted in Chapter 5. Third, men control decisions about technology, as that term is commonly understood. This third factor is the topic of this chapter.

Not only does the economic success of the Mondragon cooperatives rest on women's unpaid labor in the home, but gender stratification itself is built into and reflects manufacturing technology and its administrative structure. Both organization and administration of work in the Mondragon co-ops are similar to those of other industrial societies. Engineering education, as in the past, can serve as one conduit for patriarchal forms and the maintenance of gender stratification during times of rapid technological change. This traditional and hierarchical organization of technology stands in contradiction to the ideology and core elements of the cooperative structure of Mondragon, including the Polytecnica, which offers technical and engineering education.

First, a note about the concept of science and technology. Most feminists interested in such things write about gender and science, rather than technology. Many of the arguments are applicable to both, but there are also differences. Technology is not the application of scientific knowledge, as the texts so often state. Science generally, not always, follows technology, explaining what the technician, the engineer, the craft worker, or the farmer has been able to do. In Renaissance Italy, for example, engineers threw up domes in many styles and configurations. Some stayed up, some didn't. The scientific explanations for the successes came after, not before, the act. Since the development of science-based industries at the turn of the century these distinctions become more difficult to make. (Noble 1977)

In the United States today, although there is much overlap between science and technology, between, say, physics and engineering, one can see class and cultural differences. Engineering remains a route for upward mobility from the working class, and fights yet against the blue-collar image in which it is held. The two fields have different cultures, and they attract and shape a different practitioner. One MIT survey revealed that those in the sciences and the humanities shared similar values, but those in engineering held values similar to those in business (Snyder 1971). Ed Layton (1969) defines the difference this way: Science wants to know, engineering wants to do. Science may thus appear the more socially constructed of the two, although that is hard to say. Because of the greater extent of physical products and apparatuses in engineering, however, I believe it runs less risk of exposure as gender ideology. It is more important to me to make visible the gendering of engineering.

But in Basque culture more than perhaps most other industrial societies, the two are blended.

Gender in the History of Basque Technology

To my knowledge, there is no source material on gender in the history of Basque technology, and my awareness of works on the history of Basque technology in general is limited indeed. Much of this section is therefore speculative, with only tentative suggestions about how things went.

Both church and state affect technology in Euskadi. The Spanish state and its military institutions, consuming and influencing Basque technical ingenuity, play a special role in mingling technology with masculinity. Both church and state have gendered relations in an authoritarian form, silencing women's sexuality, forcing men's, compartmentalizing dialogues about family concerns from those of workplace and political institutions.

Basque culture is not simply innocent victim of all this. Its own traditions and institutions may be more egalitarian than those of the Spanish, but as del Valle et al. (1985) note, Basques, like Spaniards, use gender difference as a central structural principle. The more obvious effect on the development of technology is again that of military institutions.

Spanish scientific tradition, often led by Basques, focuses on the practical, on business and technology rather than pure science. The scientific community criticizes Spain still for its low level of support for pure research. Reviewing several recent works on Spanish science, Thomas Glick (1970) notes the traditional explanation: the eighteenth-century church feared a secular scientific elite or intelligentsia, and thus prevented its formation. Glick, however, finds more credence in recent fears, those the dictator Franco had for a secular scientific elite up to 1939, when his government systematically destroyed it after the Spanish civil war. Public higher education was denied the Basques in particular for decades after. Moreover, in Spain one sees the "catholicization of science." Opus Dei, a conservative Catholic lay order, secret until recent years, controls the Spanish Higher Council for Scientific Research (Glick 1970). Opus Dei also controls some important scientific/technical educational institutions in Euskadi. Glick and others are concerned for the effect on science; I am concerned for the fundamental conservative and restrictive concept of women's role. The two issues are, of course, joined (Harding 1986).

Historically, technological development in Euskadi as elsewhere is related to the militarization of major social institutions. Formal education was an affair of the church, where men and women took some part. Through the Middle Ages, however, during the period of nation building, militarization of European monasteries often meant the masculinization of education (Noble forthcoming). In the premodern age in Euskadi, also, monasteries were subject to similar masculinizing forces, although perhaps later and in more moderate form (R. Collins 1986).

Preindustrial Basque technical and scientific societies, scholars, and entrepreneurs rivaled and sometimes led those elsewhere in Europe (Garcia-Diego 1984, 1985a, 1985b). Basque hydraulic machinery in general, Villareal's water-driven forge hammers in particular, had no parallel (Villareal 1973; Garcia-Diego 1985a), for example. Also of note is Villareal's interest in mechanics and the history of mathematics, and his concern for the forest soil that supplied fuel for his iron works (Glick 1975).

Basque entrepreneurs and engineers played no small part in the yeasty period before the Industrial Revolution, traveling to and from centers in Europe, Russia, and the New World. As elsewhere, these were men of knowledge and craft skill. And both knowledge and skill were of use to armies as well as to trade. The first Iberian foundries were located in Euskadi (Urdangarin 1982) and Basque firearms equipped the armies of Europe against each other (Larrañaga 1981). The growth and development of modern Basque capitalism and industry were heavily dependent on Spanish military budgets. State contract money financed Viscaya in particular (Harrison 1983).

Although Euskadi does not now have its own army, nor do

the cooperatives make weapons, the Spanish environment is saturated with military tradition. The predominance of military institutions has been particularly marked in Spain (Childs 1982), and, as in the rest of Western Europe, the first technical schools were military academies (see articles by Barrios Gutiérrez, Baquer, and O'Dogherty Sanchez in *Temas de historia militar*, 1982). Most engineering education took place in such institutions; Basque schools of engineering are a very recent phenomenon. Spanish and U.S. armed forces continue today to maintain a masculinizing influence in Euskadi. Basque feminist scholar Zubillaga (1987) outlines the contemporary influence of military institutions on the organization of work, industry, and the related material and cultural condition of women in Basque society. The economy and organization of technology in Euskadi, as in other industrialized countries, are influenced by military institutions in ways that favor men of each class over women (see Chapter 4). This is particularly true of the acquisition of technical craft and knowledge.

Basque engineering, like engineering elsewhere, is a predominantly masculine activity. However, one characteristic that still divides Basque engineering from Spanish is the emphasis on practice, combining theory with application. This approach did not suit the Spanish nobility, including the military elite, which organized most Spanish engineering education. Although the Spanish deemphasized pure science and research, abstraction and drill versus hands-on practice typified Spanish and other European engineering education. Some attribute early successes in Basque civil engineering and design, and in the rich interplay of science, economics, crafts, and agriculture (Tellechea Idigoras 1985), to this value and skill of both hand and mind (Garcia-Diego 1985a, 1985b). Although still a masculine affair, Basque engineering culture persists in its nonelitist approach to technical, craft, and intellectual skill. This aspect of Basque culture, and our theories, lead us to believe that at Mondragon, organization, administration, and the very tools of manufacturing itself would take a different, more participatory form. How is it that the technology, including the organization of work, is not radically different in these worker-owned and -controlled firms?

Authoritarian Technics

Copreci and a few other Mondragon cooperatives now experiment with alternatives to the assembly-line organization of work described in Chapter 6. They have introduced work teams, skill sharing, and rotation of tasks (Thomas and Logan 1981). By and large, however, gender stratification and other aspects of the organization of work appear in their familiar forms for manufacturing, and I saw little difference in machine technics. Equipment was locally made, or imported from Germany, England, Japan, and the United States. Ecology is of little more interest to most than it is in Spain in general, but interest is growing.

Many workers in management strongly believe, if unfortunately, that Taylorist methods are most efficient and that the world market determines the shape of technology. Thus, the capitalist market, they believe, will force the cooperatives to follow the traditional organization of work, and to automate.

Managers themselves have noted an increase in the authority of professional training among members of the cooperatives (Perez de Callaja 1982). Today, most agree, it takes a technical degree or a degree in economics to perform the complicated work of managing, directing, making decisions. One of the directors I interviewed remembered fondly the early days of the co-ops, when "we were all in it together." But now the director, who is giving up considerable salary by staying in the cooperatives, perceives lower-level workers as ungrateful, wanting only security rather than the participation and responsibility that come with cooperativism.

Although they themselves elect managers with professional degrees, workers voiced resentment over a distant management that moves them aorund from job to job, increases or decreases work, speeds it up or slows it down. Attendance at the yearly meetings of the General Assembly of all workers is dwindling, and there is a move to require workers to attend or have their pay docked. Some workers oppose other management plans, such as to restrict "proselytizing" (to create unions, generally) for instance, or to extend the pay ratio to 5:1 (Asamblea 1986).

125

Conversation about the co-op structure was always lively. Managers again and again outlined the structure of the co-op, the democratic way the General Assembly elected managers, how the Social Council represented all sectors of the workplace. They spoke with pride of the founder, Fr. Arizmendi, who insisted on worker ownership and control, that workers could not only manage but be their own "bankers" as well (Johnson and Whyte 1982). But when I asked if and how workers were consulted on new technologies, that was a different matter.

I questioned managers and professionals about worker participation in technological decision-making, about ways this important exercise in industrial democracy might produce a "different" technology. The question was not a good one; it was answered with assurances they are moving rapidly to "catch up"—produce a higher ratio of engineers to technicians and follow the path of other industrialized countries. Development follows traditional models in other ways. I asked at Ikerlan, the high-tech R&D co-op, how they developed new technologies, software in this case, and about worker input into design. The director reported that they work only with other co-op management, or management of other client firms (the most recent member is IBM), not with other workers, to develop new computer systems. Management alone defines the need for new systems.

Everywhere, managers with professional technical degrees in fields such as engineering or economics told me workers didn't know enough to make these decisions. "Neither the General Assembly nor the Social Council has any say on this. . . . The Social Council deals with it [technological change] only if there are serious labor market consequences." Political conservatives, liberals, and radicals alike saw no decisions to be made. "Technological decisions are made by no one but the market," said one. "Technological change is imposed by the market. . . . Development is always due to need. . . . The market imposes these decisions. We have no choice. We can only control the consequences," said another. According to a third, "To compete in a capitalist market, we have to adopt the same Tayloristic practices which cheapen labor, since that is the most efficient way."

There seemed little interest in the influence of nonmarket factors on design and production—military needs, for example, or the fetishism of MIT engineers (Noble 1984). Such factors inhibit a more efficient civilian technology (Melman 1987).

Given my earlier work on the culture of engineering, and the use of math testing as a filter, I was most interested in cooperative technical education. Forces similar to those affecting manufacturing technology influence the organization of engineering education at the co-ops. The Polytecnica curriculum follows the French model, the history of which is described in chapter 4. Basque engineering students are accepted, in part, on the basis of high school math grades. When I asked if some other, or additional criteria might be more productive, I received the same answer I did in the United States (Hacker 1983a): "There aren't enough places and we have to use some objective criteria for choice."

The best graduate training is considered that obtained in more "advanced" countries. I asked if students might not come back with an elitist rather than a cooperativist ideology. At Ikerlan I was told "engineers don't have an ideology." Finally, the entry of Spain into the Common Market will strengthen the tendency toward standardized training. All engineering schools will be subject to the same requirements, to further the "free flow of intellectuals" from one country to another, according to law. On the other hand, the more liberal provisions for equal opportunity required by the Common Market countries are now applicable within Spain and Euskadi.

Democratic Technics

One can also see ways the cooperative structure does influence both machine and social technics. One manager told me the co-ops follow a path different from that taken by the United States and Japan, "where everything is done by machine." Another pointed out that during technological change, technicians are retrained rather than replaced: "They know the machines. They understand the process."

Some imported designs are modified to allow more worker decision-making, and to fit the smaller scale, say, of the civilian-oriented machine tool market. Management fear and suspicion of workers seem virtually absent, and no one explicitly endorsed gender stratification. Jobs are not yet so tightly linked to degrees; the distance between shop floor and management is not so great. Polytecnica students work on the line in factories, to help with expenses, but also to "learn the work of others." This practice fosters cooperative ideals as well.

Asked, "What would you say is the biggest difference between engineering education in the Polytecnica and a U.S. university?" the engineering director at this institution replied, "$10,000 a year." But he noted other differences. Engineering students at the elite U.S. institution where he studied were so competitive no one feared they would share information; examiners could use the honor system. At the co-ops, sharing begins before students reach the door. Classes are less formal, and there is comradely joshing between faculty and students. Women in 1986 had risen to 14 percent of enrollment, and 4 percent in higher engineering education, up considerably from 3 percent and 0 percent, respectively, in 1980. A new program in computer science attracts many more.

Hands-on, visual, and spatial training, downplayed in the United States decades ago, much to the dismay of some (see Ferguson 1977), still play an important role in the education of the polytechnic student at Mondragon: "Too much abstraction alone is not a good idea" (see also Cooley 1986; Rosenbrock 1977).

The Mondragon Polytecnica is structured as a cooperative, directed by staff, students, and participating firms. A major purpose is not, as was true for engineering education in Europe and the United States (Hacker 1983a), to create officers or bureaucrats. Yet its curriculum is modeled largely on the French, and the best students go abroad for their graduate education. Others with management and professional skills obtained elsewhere enter the system directly, say, at Ikerlan or the Business Division of the Caja, and may do so bearing an ideology at a variance with cooperative goals.

The new technocratic belief in the superiority of professional knowledge, particularly in the area of technology, stands in contradiction to the participatory and democratic philosophy of the cooperatives. As the technical and professional is gendered masculine, it meshes with gender stratification rather than equality. The strong emphasis on equality, however, provides a counterinfluence to both technocratic administration and traditional patterns of gender.

Contradictions

Cooperativist and egalitarian elements in Basque culture are currently in tension with changes in a more authoritarian direction. The cooperatives seek to balance workplace democracy with the demands of the market, and to strengthen cooperative participation, but only for men— without changing patterns of family and work. Women continue to bear a double burden. Motherhood is expected to be their primary occupation, but many enter nontraditional jobs, demanding jobs, and careers as well. Celibacy and age of marriage are increasing, as they do in economic hard times; fertility is falling in Gipuzkoa province especially. Gipuzkoa province, where Mondragon is located, is reportedly the most "Basque like" of all, in language, culture, and decentralization of industry. Arregui (1986) attributes part of these demographic changes to general modernization trends, including a structural and ideological shift on women's role in the family. For women, it is possible that these changes signal the development of contradictions similar to those Stacey (1987) finds among employed women in Silicon Valley—an attempt to distance themselves from feminism and other political struggles while fighting for more egalitarian family roles.

In the cooperatives, a manufacturing technology and a working-class culture, where craft and technical skills are gendered masculine, is shifting to management by a new, schooled, professional-technical, and in some ways more subtly masculine, culture and organization. These changes would subordinate most men and almost all women to managemet by the new professional class (Cockburn 1983). Contradictions are never so visible as during periods of rapid change. Mondragon offers a chance to observe conflicts over concepts of gender and technology in a unique instance of industrial workplace democracy.

Elsewhere, technocratic administration (Heydebrand 1985) features horizontal and vertical differentiation, high technology, decentralization, teams and quality circles, temporary projects, and job rotation. Heyderbrand suggests that the crisis of neocapitalism, contradictions between capitalism and democracy, transforms bureaucratic organization to technocratic administration. This appears to offer more participation to workers, but may yield more authoritarian control instead. An example is the sense of belonging to a family, as fostered among young women workers in the electronics industry (Grossman 1980).

These changes have many sources. The contemporary transition to technocratic administration, like most management innovations, is generally modeled on changes in military institutions during and since World War II. Operations research, systems analysis, and new forms of managerial control all have military roots (Edwards 1985, 1986b; Hacker 1988; Hoos 1972; Lilienfeld 1978; Noble 1984). Although characterized by constant interaction between civilian and military, much of the development of technology, including industrial management, has been stimulated by military institutions (Smith 1985). One route for the transmission of these anticooperative technologies—gender stratification and other hierarchies in the organization of work—to civilian industry is through technical and engineering education, which has itself, as noted in Chapter 4, been greatly influenced by military interests and values (Noble 1977; Hacker and Hacker 1987).

The influence of military institutions on technocratic forms of industrial education and organization may only partially explain the lack of fully democratic technics in the cooperatives, the persistence of gender stratification and hierarchical forms of work in these self-managed firms of Mondragon. But military influence on the organization of work and family is largely ignored. This situation suggests

130

areas for study—for example, the history of new technologies and management models deployed by the cooperatives; whether or not the entry of women in fields such as computer science will be accompanied by gender stratification at Mondragon as it has in the United States (Kraft and Dubnoff 1983); whether or not the patriarchal household remains for all practical purposes, the basic economic unit.

Gender Inequality and Feminist Activity

The feminist literature commonly draws attention to the ways gender shapes and mirrors scientific and technical knowledge and organization, from the scientific revolution to the social construction of computer textbooks (see Cohn 1987; Haraway 1981–82; Harding 1986; Keller 1985; Merchant 1980; Rothschild 1983; Smith 1974; Sørensen 1984). Some suggest ringing postmodernist directions (Haraway 1985). As noted above, most feminist scholarship deals with science rather than technology, our focus here. Recent European conferences on women and technology (Lytje et al. 1985; Dahms et al. 1986) further these investigations on the influence of gender. Only the rare feminist analysis, however, and almost none of the workplace democracy literature, investigates the role of military institutions in industry, or their implications for gender and other forms of stratification. Yet military institutions play a key role in both gender and technology; they provide the framework and the language with which we think about both, including the language of engineering and management.

To many, the structure of the patriarchal family and women's primary responsibility therein is a given, as is men's control of scientific and technical knowledge and skill. As discussed earlier (Chapter 4), both emerge with the needs of military institutions. Today, we face a matter-of-fact acceptance of these basic gendered spheres, even while we work toward radically different institutions. This cannot last for long.

In the Mondragon cooperatives, women officers and

members of boards deeply adhere to the belief that cooperativism is much more humane and productive than either monopoly capitalism or authoritarian socialism. They recognize problems of equality for women within the system, but place priority on the continued capability of the cooperatives to create new jobs, in a country now suffering 30 percent unemployment in private industry. Managers do, however, perceive diminishing enthusiasm for the cooperative project among lower-level workers.

Few women cooperative workers participate in technological research, development, or maintenance. Most operate machinery as production workers, rather than contribute as craft, technical, or scientific workers, or as managers. One production worker, who would not call herself an activist, chafed under what she saw as a distant and disinterested management. I asked if she could speak out on these concerns at the General Assembly meeting. "No, I don't feel comfortable doing that," she replied. When I asked her why, she said, "The bosses speak a different language. They stand up there and read these things I don't understand—'economy, productivity'—and so on." I asked her what she would like to say if she could. "I have no say," she responded. Professional presentation and language further mystify a technology not given to participatory control.

A sizable number of women in the city are active in both peace and feminist issues, and strongly confront administrative authority at the cooperatives. At dinner one night with cooperative workers and women who worked for private firms in Mondragon, they persisted in telling me, to my initial disbelief, that the cooperatives treated them the same way the capitalists would. This was not what I wanted to hear. It must be different, I would say, when the workers own and manage the means of production. No different at all, they would say; maybe a little more security, but at whose expense? You're supposed to stop thinking about the unemployed. But, I would argue, the profits don't go into the pockets of a few. They are returned to the community's needs (I had, after all, done my homework). What needs? they queried. Well, education. "But what are we taught? Not to question the system."

These workers, representing about 10 percent of the cooperatives' work force, spoke of a "professional" mentality on the part of management that excludes most people's participation in practice (Asamblea 1986). Management agrees this is a problem (Perez de Callaja 1982). Feminists and other activists stated they did not feel excluded from, but lacked interest in, management as currently structured. This reflects perhaps the most subtle form of exclusion. One said:

> If I went in and said, "Oh, cooperativism is good" and so on, I could be put up [for a higher position]. But I don't want to do that. We want the system to change [To what?] To be more responsive, to lead to a better life. Yes, people have money and security and live very well. But they are not happy. Work is not all. But then, what is happiness? We must all think about it.

They argued for a change in society. Some grudgingly saw the cooperatives as a possible first step in a social revolution; others saw the cooperatives as hopelessly traditional, especially in their notion of women and the family. They take an active part in the evening ritual, talking, arguing, and playing all at once. They reach out in newsletters, put up friends from other countries, organize demonstrations, have dinners, care for children. Some are married, some will never marry. They command respect. Their resistance on a day-to-day level, as we saw in Chapter 6, articulates and challenges contradictions between hierarchical organizations and the concentration of power in scarce technical knowledge, and the principles of a participatory democracy that includes both men and women.

Race and Ethnicity

Some equate the principles of cooperative organization with those of feminism (Rothschild 1987), and in principle the argument has merit. In practice, however, as we have seen, not all feminist organizations are collective, and even radical movements for social change bog down without an explicit focus on gender and eroticism (Phillips 1983). It will not benefit women much to be managed by men of their own class (Feldberg 1981).

What is true for gender applies to race and ethnicity. Mondragon spokespeople report the same proportion of non-Basques, (20 percent) in the co-ops as in the community. But data for these and other comparisons do not exist. A former manager, now college professor, says those who moved up from Spain for work have now chosen to move back; non-Basque migration is now, during slack times, outward rather than inward.

There are enough stories of very "democratic" cooperatives in the United States that turn out to be otherwise. One of Oregon's plywood cooperatives, for instance, goes Mondragon one better. Its 1:1 pay ratio—all workers earn the same—and its democratic decision-making apply, however, only to the exclusively white male members.

Cooperative and democratic self-management are often not extended beyond the dominant gender/ethnic group. And so these goals must be addressed specifically, incorporated into principles of self-management. The variety of experiences of different peoples leads to fresh perspectives and approaches to the whole of the matter (Hooks 1981; de Lauretis 1987; Harding 1986).

Thus, when people begin a cooperative, democratic participation must be ensured for all, goals for gender and ethnicity coequal with those of class. If whites or men have more skill and experience in certain areas, they can teach others, not assume leadership on the basis of that skill and experience. Further, a truly democratic structure would balance power such that a different definition of useful skill comes into existence.

Conclusion: Social Change toward Cooperative Society

Cooperatives are similar to traditional firms in gender stratification and in machine and social technologies, although they are somewhat less capital intensive. Some research finds cooperatives, in the Pacific Northwest for example, no better than traditional firms. Some are worse, in terms of hard and repetitious labor, dangerous work, and poorly designed equipment and machinery. Greenberg (1986) cites the difficulty of working within a hostile or nonsupportive society. Wherever the cooperative in existing industrial society, I suggest that major obstacles to democratic participation lie in the gendered structure of design and technology, including models of technological and managerial manufacturing.

Writings about Mondragon—whether the scholarly literature of industrial relations (e.g., Greenberg 1986), feminist works (e.g., Ferguson 1984), or leftist intellectual and movement literature (e.g., Lindenfeld 1986)—cite this system of worker-owned and -managed producer cooperatives as impressive in its degree of democratic structure and process. I have so cited it myself (Hacker 1985). A closer look at Mondragon, and conversation with women workers and Basque feminists, reveals the distance even Mondragon must travel to become a workplace democracy, fully selfmanaged by all its workers, paid and unpaid.

Although more widely shared among men in Mondragon than in most large cooperatives (Rothschild and Whitt 1986), technical and professional knowledge and skill are increasingly concentrated among a few in administrative positions, predominantly men. Family and child-care skills are concentrated among women, or men have distanced themselves from those activities. It goes against the grain of the cooperatives to suggest that only a few can or should master any set of skills. The logical extension of this approach encompasses both workplace skills and domestic skills. At the same time, it is unwise to accept any skills as valuable without examining their roots—and asking what it means that technical skills have their origins in military institutions while domestic skills have their origins in lifesustaining activities of families and communities.

Efforts toward worker self-management—all workers taking equal part in a democratic, nonhierarchical process to make decisions about important dimensions of their work—take place in context from reform to revolution (Gunn 1984; Kravitz 1974; Giese 1982). Those cooperative efforts that, as in China, form part of a general movement of opposition, a movement toward social transformation, are not as easily co-opted as those that aim merely for reform or for greater gain for their own members. Gunn (1984) outlines specific dimensions of a self-managed firm, but insists it must be set in a new society. Neither existing socialist nor capitalist societies provide supportive environments for worker/community management. According to Gunn, the first step toward democratic society is to reintegrate the left, labor, feminist, and other progressive movements into nonreformist programs of broad appeal. One of these programs can be worker self-management. In a politics of linkages, workers and citizenry, factory *and* neighborhood council, can plan cooperative and democratic workplaces. But this will progress only in the context of a society addressing problems of gender, race, and ethnicity. In that context, child care is a major issue.

Community responsibility for child care and other unpaid women's work requires a commitment of resources that even the socialist state is loath to give up (Nazzari 1983). In addition to domestic labor, women provide much of the infrastructure of neighborhood networks and valuable services such as shopping or volunteer work in education, health, and other areas (Sacks and Remy 1984; Tilly 1981; Daniels 1985; Glazer 1984). This is true in Euskadi as well (del Valle 1983; del Valle et al. 1985). Liberation may release energy for productivity, but women have a right to shape their own lives while society needs this work done. But new resources are not likely to come into existence by wishing it were so, disengaging, or taking action, say, for one's own child alone. Individual action is effective only when joined with collective action, as when a struggle for one's own children's welfare becomes a struggle for the welfare of the children of the community (P. Collins 1986). With family, as with community life, if the forms of resistance we take are not now collective, cooperative, and oppositional, they can become so (Tilly 1986).

Of the many feminisms I have worked with, social anarchist feminism seems most compatible with these requirements for collective action (Kornegger 1975). Nonhierarchical social relations require new participatory and environmentally sensitive technologies. Social anarchist feminism suggests a decentralized form of coordination, federations of workplaces, communities, and cultures, as opposed to today's highly centralized bureaucratic administration of state, organization, and corporation. As Rothschild and Whitt (1986) demonstrate for social anarchism in general, a durable order emerges from trial and error of people addressing their community needs.

A common social anarchist goal is organization without hierarchy—cooperative, participatory work and leisure, autonomous communities, federations of communities as opposed to nation-states, with rotating leadership, determined by lot. (Why not?) In such a perspective, community responsibility for child care and other home work is explicitly a priority, articulated theoretically and in practice. The person rather than the traditional family household can be the basic economic unit. When the family is the economic unit, much of women's labor remains unpaid. The practice of paying a man a family wage so that he can support his dependents ensures their dependency, and also that of the marketplace (Lehrer 1987). Whether workpoints, wages, land, or other resources, what is distributed to the family as a unit strengthens its patriarchal structure (Stacy 1983). Ideally, resources for child care and other work and play would be distributed on the basis of need, not ability to work or pay (Nazzari 1983).

There are collective models of child care, but these do not guarantee a resistance consciousness. Basque patterns of child care can be gendered and traditional or degendered and egalitarian. Cuadrilla and kibbutz provide models for community child rearing, but these will remain alternative or accommodating to current institutions, rather than oppositional, to the extent gender is maintained.

This is not an argument for the deeroticised relationships noted by Talmon (1972) in the kibbutz, or the reserve among the Basques (del Valle et al. 1985). These patterns have merits, such as the strong bonds of solidarity and identification. But also I argue for new relations that more easily include the erotic along with the collective, and do not use erotic power to build or maintain structures of dominance. The family varies from culture to culture on the meaning of eroticism. We can move away from community patterns that gender eroticism and link it with power or fear and humiliation. We can move toward those forms that infuse egalitarian relations with eroticism. Erotic experience, like technological experience, should not be so scarce, so hard to get for the many, and thus so exploitable. We would more likely express playfulness and mutuality in new technologies if we lived in a society in which eroticism was part of reciprocal, egalitarian relations (Hacker 1987d).

Strategies of nonviolence also follow from social anarchist feminist goals and methods. Nonviolence requires, for example, that information be shared widely; secrecy is said to be the hallmark of violent organizations (Lakey 1987). Decision-making by consensus requires that everyone take part and take responsibility, or agree to stand aside; one is not overridden by a majority. Especially among feminists, but also in Basque society, with its collective social networks, we find models for the capabilities of nonviolent resistance such as the effective use of the general strike.

Cooperative workplaces form part of a new democratic society—but they cannot stand alone. The current discussion of cooperative workplaces does not go far enough. To begin, political scientists suggest that notions of democracy that we apply to the governmental sphere be extended to include private industry. As citizens choose their form of government and elect its leadership, workers also can choose their form of work and elect its management (Pateman 1970). Others argue that this is not sufficient for a democratic society. In the case of large multinationals like IBM it is clear that all the people, not merely those who work for the company, have a stake in the policies of that workplace (Graubard 1984).

Large or small, the workplace depends on and thus should be guided by the community rather than the member/worker alone. When the community is perceived as the collective of its members, not patriarchal households or families, women will enter workplace decision-making as men engage in daily life decisions about the care and rearing of children. For

Mondragon, the relationship between the cooperative and those outside, primarily women, is as yet unexplored. There is more to the story of cooperatives than efficiency, jobs, and pay; more than issues of ownership and control of the means of production; more than the question of socialist revolution, as Stacey (1983) has shown. I agree with Ehrenreich et al. (1986), who say it is again time to "rethink pleasure as a human goal and reclaim it as a human project" (p. 208). Our collective efforts with respect to gender and technology can also address the erotic, and can be therefore the more pleasurable.

John Street (1983) extends the usual critique of cooperative workplaces, addressing questions Marx concerned himself with, such as the purpose of work itself. Work can be an expression of human creativity and a source of freedom, but these worthy goals are unlikely to be met unless joined with those of feminists (Feldberg 1981; Gunn 1984; Acker 1982; Pateman 1983; Wajcman 1983; Cockburn 1983, 1985). Examples of feminist goals that make a difference are a participatory and degendered technology and eroticism, community responsibility for child care, gender and race liberation, and democratic and participatory organizations that do not depend on women's unpaid labor in home and community. Including these goals, articulating and giving them priority, might move socialism, communism, and social anarchism more truly toward their stated aims.

CHAPTER 8

Conclusion Stories

A major barrier to social change from the bottom up is our tendency to go home after work and stay there. One recent evening, I called part of a list for a political/social get-together, and 90 percent of the people answered their phones. This made life easier, but it set me to thinking about Mondragon, and San Sebastian, where for at least an hour or two a night, everyone was on the streets, chatting, gossiping, passing news, talking politics. The evening ritual is not peculiar to Basque country, but the intense intertwining of the social and the political is characteristic of the culture (Zubillaga 1987).

Charles Tilly has written an elegant book, *The Contentious French* (1986), which documents the public actions of French people, from seventeenth-century gatherings of "women of the dregs" protesting grain shortages and taxes for the army rather than the community, to twentieth-century workplace strikes and mass demonstrations against capital and the nation-state. He reminds us that "ordinary people have the urge to resist" (p. 131), with good reason: state and army advance at their expense. Historic protest against, and resistance to, the state, then to capital, were not "disorders." They followed certain patterns and repertoires, changed with the times, with innovation and practice, and made use of the stuff of everyday life. Far from a disorderly mob, Tilly's rich mosaic shows a people in action, performance, making it up as they go, learning new and more effective ways to resist concentration of power.

Thre are many ways to be contentious. Once, I was talking in class about direct action when a student said, "Well, like what would you do? I went in to see about jobs, and the university has these books, say, 'Jobs for Men' and 'Jobs for Women.'" Well! But it was an example. One could

140

reason with people, point out that it was illegal, or file suit. Or one could create some direct action. That afternoon several of us went over to the university employment office, and it really was as the student had said—no, worse. The "Jobs for Women" book had a big pink flower pasted on its cover. And the work in "Jobs for Men" paid more. I left the motorcycle running outside the door, and we "seized" the books. Two women blocked the door while I sped down the hall with the stuff, jumped onto the bike, and rode off into the distance—actually, to the doorstep of the affirmative action officer, who was an acquaintance, and to whom we later explained what had happened. The books were quickly and quietly integrated.

The first time I did a witch action (news of which had spread to Houston in the 1960s from New York's Redstockings) was at a meeting of the American Association for the Advancement of Science. Two young women proposed the idea to those of us who had come, rather primly, to a meeting to see what "women could do" about the way men had organized science and research. When they suggested a hex, we lost most of the crowd. I asked if there wasn't something else for those of us with sweaty palms. You'll love it, they said, trimming and stitching the black capes with which we later flew into the award symposium. The hex was good poetry, I thought. The part about the misuse of science was picked up by AAAS's magazine, *Science*. I remember being surprised that they understood the point.

Such guerrilla theater, spurred by wild and outlandish worldviews, was in the air as described in *Sisterhood Is Powerful* (Morgan 1970). In public actions, we illustrated our perspective and had a party at the same time. Some people became very serious about all this, especially the religious part, and some went winging off into the ether, generally missing their neighbors. But usually one can think of something to do that engages people, is productive, and gets the juices going at the same time.

Once, in Iowa, we heard that a beauty pageant would take place in Iowa State University's C. Y. Stevens Auditorium. As if that wasn't bad enough, educational television was planning to broadcast it live. We couldn't decide what to do.

The days of anger at women being judged for "pretty" were waning; we really didn't care. A beauty pageant seemed a dinosaur from the past. Still, it was an affront and there we were. Along with traditional feminist groups and organizations, we took action compatible with the loosely articulated liberal feminist framework. We met with officials who were surprised we would object—the pageant would help girls, and after all, the auditorium was there. We asked the television representatives what they thought was educational about the pageant. They seemed embarrassed, and spoke of the older rural folks who wanted it on the air.

We met with the women contestants who explained (once we got past talent) how the experience would teach them pride and self-confidence in their appearance; no, they hadn't thought why this was especially important for women, why one should wear a bathing suit to get such experience, or that men might need the experience more. Nor did the contestants particularly object to being measured like a side of beef or answering questions about being out of the country lately. An important factor, however, was the scholarship given the winner.

We did our research, and then asked corporate sponsors why, if they wanted to help women, did they not open up their corporate structures to women (petroleum, plumbing, cosmetics)? Why not open career ladders for all those clerical workers in the oil industry (95 percent of their female workforce at the time), or encourage women to enter the crafts? One feebly responded that most women did not want to be plumbers. True, only 3 percent did, but only 3 percent wanted to grow up to be waitresses, too. We were so smart. But pageant preparations continued.

We changed tactics and, with additional friends from the left, took to the streets on Valentine's Day, leafleting and hollering about the corporations, their exploitation of a labor force divided by race and sex, and how they were using the pageant as a tax write-off. (This took place in the days when people would accept a leaflet and read it.)

Pah! Nothing was going to stop this pageant. So we decided to let off steam, make known how we felt and why, and have a good time. Working in different ways along different theoretical lines—left, liberal, feminist—but with as consistent an oppositional resolution as we could muster, we were indeed a motley crew; but by this time, we were also full of ideas. Couples with children, old folks, wild women, wild men, some of us costumed, painted, and frizzed, others with demands, still others with staid educational posters, showed up the night of the pageant.

Public display comes easier to some than others. Yates was splendid, leaping from crotch to crotch with her tape measure, astonishing the men who had come to buy tickets for the pageant with shouts of "Four inches! Throw 'im back!" "Six inches, OK! More like it!" or, "Wow, lookit this one—eight inches!! Awright!!" This kind of action may not fit with today's taste for the fine edge between laughter at and empathy with the opposition, but something else no doubt would.

Our hex worked quite well, too. We hexed the university and the television station. To our surprise, the transformer blew out in midperformance and the station had to cancel the broadcast.

Then we heard a rumor, one we had heard before. The university planned a $7.4 million sports stadium on ground next to the auditorium. So we hexed the land, too, and claimed the $7.4 million for child care instead. Flo Kennedy had come through the state earlier and, in response to a cautious comment that we shouldn't act when things were just in the rumor stage, said something like, "Listen, cupcake, if you don't stop it at the rumor stage, you don't stop it at all."

Anyway, it had been a great night, and so much for the pageant, we thought. The following year it was held off campus in a small building and hardly anyone went. Two years later construction of the sports stadium was under way. But, at a women's party one night about 11:00 p.m., someone burst through the door with a "Guess what!" Planning had gone awry as it happened, and the stadium, being built over a fault in the floodplain, sank several inches and would have to be torn down and reconstructed.

It was midnight by the time we delivered press releases to the media, from the instant group DARC, the Des Moines

143

Area Radical Coven. (*Ames Daily Tribune* 1974) The next day the media did some calling—to me at my office, for one—to check on the "legitimacy" of this group. Then they went ahead and publicized the news that DARC had earlier hexed the ground, took responsibility for the land shifting under the stadium, but would be happy to lift the hex when the community received $7.4 million in funds for the care of children.

☆ ☆ ☆

Tilly's point is well taken. Capital and the state will intrude where they can, and increasingly so. Resistance, especially nonviolent resistance, is not only pleasurable but necessary for a full, self-directed life, and for the well-being of the community. Tilly's view, while fresh and invigorating, also raises practical, everyday questions: Where did the people come from for these acts of collective resistance? Who were they and how did they know each other? What forms of leisure and family, what networks of communication, brought them together and facilitated their collective action?

The Basque cooperatives are a good example of alternative forms of work with potential for catalyzing resistance. But we can learn from other aspects of Basque culture as well. Basque solidarity is most remarkable. Forms of leisure are politically significant. As Peiss (1986) shows for the turn-of-the-century working woman and man in New York City, street life and celebration, nickelodeons, dances, and amusement parks are the stuff of everyday life that provide a starting point for community solidarity not necessarily basic or family. These networks are prerequisites to action against concentrations of power.

Basque street life figures large in the politics of the country. The networks of solidarity and communication are necessary ingredients for large-scale nonviolent resistance such as the general strike. During one such strike over a disappeared youth (described in Chapter 6), San Sebastian was errie in its silence. Nothing moved, nothing was sold, the streets were empty.

Such networks and patterns of communication provide a

counter to the increasing penetration of the twentieth-century state into everyday life. As for the United States, if not 25 pubs per block, we could start with a goal of at least one, a place and a time to gather and talk.

Friends and Individuals:
What a Few Can Do

But what happens in between times, when people as a group are not acting, reacting, protesting, resisting concentrations of power and authority? Small groups of friends can keep us going. It is difficult without them. The seduction of individualistic intellectual work pulls us away. As in military/bureaucratic organizations, we are supposed to focus on the next rung up, or at least stay cool, holding things together as they are, preserving order. Oppositional groups, like feminists, place values differently—on friendship, for example—which might interfere with or be merely incidental to that order.

In such times when masses do not move in the streets, the action of each one is that much more important. Perhaps, in such times, the personal idiosyncrasies of, say, a U.S. president have further-reaching consequences than when tempered by the desires of the collectivity. But so, too, for the rest of us and our activities.

In the 20 years encompassing this research, I have been impressed over and over at the accomplishments of a few. In Texas, and in Iowa, although hundreds took to the streets, generally much of the organization, education, and lively celebration was coordinated by a half-dozen people in each case, intermittently helped by 20 or 30 friends. Moving to Boston in 1975, I looked forward to seeing how larger and more sophisticated groups of activists got things done. Usually, I found a half-dozen dedicated activists helped by 20 or 30 friends.

Although no organization need last forever, keeping one going for several years may be important; working women knew where to call. Keeping friendships rich across time and space is important in and of itself. It also helps resistance, as

145

when migrant workers pass information along through chains of people who know and trust each other. Maintaining friendships in a highly mobile society is hard, a problem unknown to those who have the lifelong geographic stability I found in Mondragon. Mobile or stable, Gunn's (1984) "politics of linkages" suggests tolerance and learning to work with other oppositional groups for common goals.

Things don't always go as planned. Despite good long-term friendships, we let go, make mistakes. For example, after much training in nonviolent protest, this time over planned Junior ROTC programs from kindergarten to twelfth grade, Haysie jumped on the back of a burly teenager who was wrestling Tom, a presumed commie, to the ground. Sometimes in civil rights action in Texas our friends' homes and cars and persons were threatened or damaged. And there are (and were) some times and places when even a few friends with similar goals and values and energy are not to be found. Many of us are now in the mesh of earning a living under difficult circumstances, taking care of parents or children or both. At these times we have less to do with other working people (and the poor) whose collective voices might otherwise give us new direction. If those of us who are white find it tough and are tempted to let go, then how much greater is the temptation for those of us who are of color? Toni Cade Bambara's (1981) *Salt Eaters* shows "a bottom down below," as Melvina Reynolds put it. There is despair, but there is also a way to return, to build and rebuild ties of community.

At other times one is alone. Sometimes, when my beliefs and actions are shared by no nearby other, I have found history, literature, and ethnography illuminating, exciting, and sustaining. And in some of our wall-to-wall Anglo communities, the literature of women of color may be as close as we can get to knowing other women's worlds.

Sometimes, however, I go off on a tangent, forgetting my roots, and read, talk, and write only for other intellectuals. I try on a new style, see how it fits, and lose touch with women who work with their hands. This is very easy to do if one teaches for a living. We intellectuals tend to develop our own style, aloof from other working women's lives.

Sometimes I get restless in this professional job, feel out of touch, like I'm missing something. The work goes stale or strange. Last time that happened, I took a year off, without pay or savings, and went to Los Angeles to look for production or technical work in the electronics industry. I found none, but worked as a secretary in an engineering firm. I had had a grant for research, but the Reagan administration cut the funds. I relearned the complex skills of the clerical worker, but not fast enough. Then I learned the very different skills of unemployment in the big city. This kind of activity is not possible for or appealing to many, but there it is. I recommend it.

DEGENDERING TECHNOLOGY

The best chance we have of creating change is through getting together with others. One can learn so much and enjoy the process—in collective action. Feminist goals and processes are important for women and others in gaining access to the resources of the community, in beginning our independent shaping of ourselves. Feminism also creates a different quality of work. Hal Hartzell's (1987) book on the Hoedads shows the advantages of collective action growing out of feminist perspective. The hoedad is a tree-planting instrument, taken as symbol by these radical workers. Hartzell has lectured in my class. Women's participation, he says, gives these tree-planting cooperatives an extra edge over their private competitors. Students asked if that was because of women's traditional skills in interpersonal work. While it is true that women traditionally have good interpersonal skills, as Rothschild (1987) illustrates from small group research, all areas of women's skills develop to a particularly high degree in cooperative settings; women learn from interaction, whereas men use it to win points. Hartzell said it was the interpersonal skills, or the group's ability to learn from interaction in particular, but he added that women tend to have such different life experiences from men that they bring fresh ideas to a project. The students wanted to know if those ideas were about social organization, or about technology in the usual sense. He said "both," and gave examples of women suggesting new uses for wood by-products, and a new design for a political candidate's campaign logo. Oppositional models do exist or can be imagined, as Piercy (1976) does so well.

The Social Context of Cooperativism

As illustrated in this book, technological skill that gives access to power is largely defined as a masculine character-istic—both craft and administrative skills are identified as core elements in the concept of masculinity. Whether hard and dirty or clean and computerized, gender and power define the job (Cockburn 1983, 1985).

Gender exists only in the context of gender stratification, and who defines and controls technological skill is important. Gender stratification is a process—re-created in everyday interchange and embedded in institutions, much as E.P. Thompson (1963) shows for class. It is the fundamental process that shapes and organizes patriarchal societies, which in turn refine and develop their own particular meanings of gender stratification.

In the research-action presented in Part I, I described the characteristics of a gendered and stratified technology displayed in the organization of work at AT&T and agribusiness organizations. Historically, a gendered and stratified culture of engineering links military institutions to that organization of work. Engineering and other professional education assures eventual gendering of new skills.

Both men and women in the field of engineering, like workers in industry and soldiers in the army, experience an externally imposed discipline appropriate to a masculine and hierarchical structure, particularly a discipline over pleasure and spontaneity. This affects the shape of technological product and process. For most who take part in it, technology is a sensual, often erotic, activity. Our inclination to express ourselves in various ways runs counter to the mold. Why should we be surprised to see an erotic energy appropriate for military institutions finding its expression in technological products, administrative process, and other aspects of the labor process?

These institutions, and the gender stratification on which they rest, attempt to limit eroticism to relations of dominance and submission. The process thus captures and adapts this powerful social energy for hierarchical organizations. It helps us accommodate ourselves to existing institutions, and guides our minds and hands in the creation and use of certain kinds of technology. As an engineering student myself, I learned how much of this is not merely done *to* us, but also *by* us, as we participate in and thereby strengthen existing institutions. The liberating, degendering of eroticism is crucial to the transformation of technology, work, and society.

In this book, I have focused on new ways of thinking about gender, technology, and workplaces, contrasting these with traditional approaches. Cooperative workplaces offer one model, but one as yet incompletely integrated with a feminist and cooperative community. When we expand concepts of cooperation to include community as well as workplace, our ways of working and our technologies will change. Without changes that address hierarchies of race and gender as well as class, cooperative workplaces are democratic only for men of the dominant ethnic group. A fully self-managed, gender-equal, and democratic workplace/community can address technology and eroticism directly, in nonracist, feminist context.

Such a feminist context requires sharing a degendered scientific and technological knowledge and craft skill as widely as possible, and to people as young as possible. We could arrange preschool technology centers, perhaps modeled on Cooley's Technology Centers for the people in London. I visited one in a garage, big as a warehouse, where people experimented with new forms of transportation—electric self-charging bikes, buses to' fit both rail and road—and where they had places to work on their cars or motorcycles, and tools to work with.

Another set of models specifically designed for girls are those projects suggested by the Girls into Science and Technology (GIST) actions in England (J. Whyte 1986). Chapter 6 of this report suggests ways to teach a "girl-friendly science" in "science by doing," which involves the body for study and action—by, for instance, pretending to be a wave. Girls, especially, like to do hands-on experimental work, with models, balances, living plants, living animals (p. 99). This is one of the few programs that combines interest and action in higher-status scientific careers and occupations with blue-collar craft work.

We need alternatives to existing technologies and some say a feminist standpoint can provide such alternatives. These arguments are analyzed in Harding (1986). Some practitioners focus solely on women, for example, women on the land in southern Oregon; some, on making technologies that use women's skills to meet women's needs, from dream work to design of living spaces to creation and use of nonmetallic tools and organic gardening. Others accept that there is a worthwhile science and technology, badly distorted, but that can be transformed for and by the use of the people, particularly women (Smith 1978; Bush 1981).

Here in our city, one woman wanted a solar heater. Five of us had different skills, from carpentry to calculus (the least useful). Finding, buying, or designing material and building a heater became a social project, an opportunity to share skills. We also produced a good heating unit. I have a license to operate a HAM radio—a heavily gendered activity—and visions of progressive, feminist stations here and there.

We know that the argument for democratic technics must go beyond equal representation of men and women in skills and at work and home. We know that gender provides a major metaphor for comprehending and acting on the social and natural world, and that what we gender "feminine" is more easily controlled. One vision of a new society is a society where gender does not matter. While that vision is ideal, separatism may meanwhile be useful.

At a Stanford University seminar, I heard from women in a London women's collective who would not speak with men, even for help in home and auto repair. They were determined. If they didn't know how to fix wiring, they had no lights until they purchased tools, searched the library, and accomplished practice. An Oregon women's country living collective allowed no males, even children. Such arrangements are obviously not for all, or for all time, but can be effective solutions for some. While too removed from the social world for most of us—indeed, that is their point—these situations offer the opportunity to learn and practice technological and craft skills generally reserved for boys and men.

Mixed groups are the norm, but without separatist efforts in the past, we would all be weaker in the present. This is a difficult issue, handled cautiously, for instance, by the GIST program in England, where Whyte observed that boys do usurp technology in the classroom (see J. Whyte 1986, Chapter 2: "Edging Girls Out"). Whyte cites instances where teachers, intentional or not, allowed boys the lead. At other times, the boys simply brought their sense of entitlement with them into the classroom. In project after project, girls-only classes provided the experience they needed to learn craft, technical, and scientific skills. As we know, a separate-but-equal policy does not work, or does not work for long. For one thing, the funding is never equal. But this way of learning technical skill and knowledge can be pursued alongside the movement for reciprocal and balanced power among men and women and the search for new technologies.

Microsyster in London is a good example of a women's cooperative workplace of computer scientists, technicians, and clerical workers who provide computer assistance to the network of women's groups throughout Britain. They also publish the *Woman and Computing Newsletter*. For more information, contact Microsyster, Wesley House, Wild Court off Kingsway, London WC2B 5AU. In Europe and the United States, a strong network of women in technology coordinates and disseminates information. ISIS (1984) Women's International Information & Communication Service is an especially valuable source of names and addresses of a large number of groups concerned with various aspects of women and technology; for more, contact ISIS Italy, Via S. Maria dell'Anima 30, 00186 Roma, Italy; or ISIS Switzerland, Case Postale 50 (Cornavin), CH-1211 Geneva 2, Switzerland. For other names and addresses both in the United States and abroad, see Fuentes and Ehrenreich (1983:62–63). At this point the network comprises primarily professional and technical women—computer scientists, technicians, biologists, midwives, mathematicians, engineers, and social scientists interested in technology. Firmer links with women in vocational education would be most helpful as a first step in providing women the chance to learn from and work with women in crafts and production.

Working women in and out of unions organize around issues of technological change and pay equity, as the content of jobs changes and skills are redefined. They do so at this very moment at my university. The organization 9-to-5, the National Association of Working Women, based in Cleveland, can be a helpful resource for this information and analysis. (Their address is 614 Superior Avenue N.W., Cleveland, OH 44113.) See also Cummings and Schuck (1979) and the recent report by the National Research Council on technology and women's employment (Hartmann et al. 1986). The British GIST project network noted above seems particularly rich in people and ability, though desperately underfunded.

I suggest any study of gender and technology stay close to research and action for and with women who have the fewest resources—poor women, working-class women, women of color, women in the Third World. Information on women and technology in developing countries is available through campus Women in International Development (WID) centers. Michigan State University pursues a particularly active publishing effort: contact Office of WID, 202 International Center, Michigan State University, East Lansing, MI 48824. Once again ISIS (1984) is valuable, as is Fuentes and Ehrenreich (1983), for groups working from or for the Third World. Especially interesting because it addresses the effects of military as well as economic institutions is the American Friends Service Committee/Nationwide Women's Program (AFSC/NWP), which distributes films, kits, and other research materials. For information, write Saralee Hamilton, AFSC/NWP, 1501 Cherry Street, Philadelphia, PA 19102. A really exciting project would be to establish communication between women working in production, clerical, and technical work in the United States—at the Hewlett-Packard plant in my backyard, for instance—and their counterparts in other countries.

☆   ☆   ☆

In this chapter, I have suggested more collective action. Through some stories, I have illustrated how we might do more partying and getting together for social change, more linking of (and mediating between) our pleasures and our politics. I have recalled some actions that, for a time, created their own language and ways of changing the realities in which we live. Finally, I have listed some projects and people active in the network of women and technology.

Some of us, women from the working class, have an opportunity and gentle obligation to air our views. At this point perhaps simply being more aware of eroticism and its political power, with respect to technology, is as much as we can do. We can work together best, I think, by listening to and learning more of other working women. In particular, we need to learn how and where the interests and everyday lives of Third World women mesh with those of us in industrialized societies, and where we might make common cause among ourselves and with others (Nazzari 1983; Haraway 1985; Grossman 1980; Sacks and Remy 1984; Nash and Kelly 1982; D'Onofrio-Flores and Pfafflin 1982; Croll 1982; Tilly 1981). At the same time, organize a union, have a party, write, talk. Others need to hear from us, and it can be a kick.

RAISING HELL

A Sketch of the Sociologist as Intellectual and Activist
Sally Hacker 1936–1988

You can learn a lot about Sally's life from *Pleasure, Power, and Technology*. Autobiography, in fact, informed much of her writing. Believing you could best understand sociological results only if you knew why and how the sociologist had tackled a problem, she insisted on telling not only findings but motives and methods as integral parts of her research. Pretensions to the contrary notwithstanding, value-free sociology has more often meant values hidden than values absent. Far better to set the motives up front where the reader can judge for him or herself rather than leave them lurking in the background, all too easy to overlook, ignore, or forget. By the same token, method meant more to Sally than manipulating data. Technical virtuosity counted, but only as a step on the road from study to action. Deciding what questions mattered came first, then finding ways (not always conventional) to get the data that might provide answers. Analysis—sometimes rough and ready, sometimes as subtle and sophisticated as anything in the field—then prepared the way for the next step: putting the results in the hands of people who could use it, whether they were office workers facing automation, farm wives confronted by encroaching agribusiness, or sociologists seeking to understand technology (Hacker 1979c, 1985). Research without action—without potential to advance social justice—was not research she deemed worth doing. In her ceaseless effort to seek and destroy the roots of oppression, Sally was radical in the word's literal, and best, sense.

154

How did that happen? Surely it had something to do with being born and raised in downstate Illinois, halfway between the birthplace of American sociology's most actively radical founding father, E. A. Ross, and the town where Mother Jones lies buried (Coser 1978:301; Fetherling 1974:213–215). Devoutly Lutheran and Republican, Sally's parents encouraged her independence, to a point. Her tomboy phase lasted until age 10, when she learned that girls didn't play baseball or football, though they might become cheerleaders or major-ettes. She did both, and other things too. Thanks to Andrew Carnegie, Litchfield had a public library where you could find Freud as well as the encyclopedia. Fascinated by psychology, she looked forward to college and a career as psychoanalyst. That was not to be. Her life took a different turn when she met a sweet-talking stranger from the big city. Pregnancy, marriage, and expulsion from high school followed in rapid order. Eventually, the young family returned to Chicago, where Sally finished high school by mail and in due course discovered the city's community college system. At Amundsen Junior College she also discovered sociology. It was love at first sight.

Determined to become a sociologist, she won a scholarship to the University of Chicago—a move that ended her marriage. Working to support herself and her son Mark, she also explored an unimagined world of knowledge and began honing the research skills she needed. A graduate fellowship in survey research from the National Institutes of Mental Health supported her study at the National Opinion Research Center. Although Chicago nurtured a reputation for radical social science, little of that tradition manifested itself during the 1950s and early 1960s (Smith 1988; Coser 1978:303–306, 311–317). The stirrings of a campus only just beginning to awaken from a torpid decade sounded only the most muffled call to action. But when we married and moved to Houston in 1966, we found plenty to keep us busy in civil rights and antiwar movements, though none of it meshed with work. Sally had joined a mental health research team as evaluator (Hacker and Gaitz 1969, 1970; Hacker et al. 1972; Hacker 1973). Gerontology, however, proved more interest-ing than engaging; it inspired no action. Both of us were still writing our dissertations, Sally under Alice Rossi (Hacker

1969). One day a letter arrived, telling her about a new group that Alice had just helped form, the National Organization for Women (Hole and Levine 1971:342–343; Carden 1974:103–105). We quickly founded a Houston chapter of NOW. Sally had always been a feminist; she simply hadn't known what to call herself. The women's movement at last provided the arena in which she could fully exercise her skills and unite research and action. The rest, as they say, is history. Much of it appears in this book, but let me briefly outline the basic chronology.

Working closely with the Equal Employment Opportunity Commission during the late 1960s, Sally analyzed affirmative action plans to show decisively how conventional statistical treatments disguised sex discrimination by comparing minority women to white women, rather than women to men (Briggs et al. 1970:74–82). Sally also made sure her findings reached women working in the companies as well as NOW. Initially only one of the subjects of study, the Bell system became the target of further research; ultimately, Sally's findings strongly shaped NOW's key role in the landmark multimillion-dollar AT&T settlement of 1973 (Wallace and Nelson 1976:250).[1] Curiously, however, the lot of women in the phone company seemed not to improve very much, and she began wondering about sources of technological change and managerial uses of technological innovation. We moved to Iowa in 1970, where Sally taught sociology at Drake University in Des Moines; we quickly formed a central Iowa NOW chapter. A faculty research fellowship from the Ford Foundation allowed her to complete the analysis for her important and much-cited *Social Problems* paper on "Sex Stratification, Technology, and Organizational Change" in AT&T (Hacker 1979a; see also Hacker 1975, 1977b, 1978). Decisions about new technologies, it seemed, had as much to do with manipulating the workforce as with increasing profits.

The same Ford grant allowed Sally to study technological and social change in other Iowa industries as well: displacement of craftwork in printing and publishing, office automation in insurance, and the mechanization of farming. Agribusiness growth at the expense of family farming, in particular, sparked her concern. From that research came her incisive report on technological change and the lives of rural women, "Farming Out the Home" (Hacker 1977a). Once again, she shared her findings widely, with a broad spectrum of feminists, migrant workers, farm women, advocates of appropriate technology, academics, and rural social workers (Hacker 1979c, 1979d, 1979e, 1979f, 1980, 1982, 1983b; Hacker and Bovit 1981). Meanwhile we'd become grandparents, Sally learned roofing and tried communal living, and a motorcycle became her preferred mode of transport (Hacker 1976). She moved easily between roles as disparate as college teacher and witch, civil libertarian and radical activist. All this and more helped make the early and mid-1970s the yeasty time so vividly portrayed in *Pleasure, Power, and Technology*

Increasingly, technological change seemed to Sally the central engine of modern social change; unlike many, though, she refused to view technology as an independent factor. Rather she saw it embedded in a matrix of social groups, relations, and processes. Technology, in other words, became a fit subject for sociological analysis as both cause and effect of social change. To balance then common questions about the impact of technology on society, Sally started asking about the social shaping of technology—how human purposes and values, interests and motives, institutions and actions, produce our technologies. Circumstances have changed dramatically in the past decade or so, but few scholars were asking such questions in the mid-1970s when the sociology of technology scarcely existed as a field of study. Guided by what she had already learned about technological innovation in the Bell system, Sally resolved to study engineering. Engineers appeared to occupy a crucial nexus in the corporate creation and deployment of new technologies. That made the next step clear: find out what made engineers tick. In 1975, with help from the Mellon Foundation, she set off for MIT to begin doing just that. She audited engineering classes, talked with students and engineers, interviewed faculty members, and read widely. Continuing her research while teaching sociology at Oregon

State University from 1977 onwards, she formally enrolled as an engineering student. Later she even took a secretarial job with an engineering firm.

Engineering was never to Sally merely machines and buildings or an occupational field lacking female practitioners. It was those things, of course, but it was also ideology and culture—ways of looking at the world and ways of molding society. Her angle of vision widened to include past as well as present, the social shaping of engineering practice as well as the internal structure of the engineering profession (Hacker 1979b, 1981a, 1983a, 1983c, 1983d, 1984; Hacker and Starnes 1983). By the late 1970s, Sally was finding less scope for the kind of activism she had earlier practiced. But taking advantage of a quiet decade, she reflected more deeply on her findings and shared her insights with a wider audience. Several themes assumed growing prominence in her thinking as the decade progressed. One was the largely overlooked past and present influence of military institutions on the organization, ideology, and tasks of engineering, and through engineering, on work and society (S. Hacker and B. Hacker 1983, 1984; Hacker 1986a; B. Hacker and S. Hacker 1987). A second theme centered on work itself, the labor process, and the quest for a democratic workplace as affected by technological change (Hacker 1981b, 1983d, 1987a, 1987b, 1987c, 1988; Hacker and Starnes 1983; Hacker and Hacker 1987). More recently, a third theme increasingly came to the fore: technology's aesthetic and erotic dimensions. "The whole field of engineering," she said in a 1987 interview, "is shot through with passion and excitement" (Middendorff 1987:3). She was just beginning to explore what that implied (Hacker 1986b, 1987d; Hacker et al. 1985). All these themes figure largely in *Pleasure, Power, and Technology*.[2]

Sally looked forward to the coming decade, believing, as many of us do, that a time for action is building again. But this time it will have to be without her. Sally would have led, as she always did, though seldom seeing herself as leader. Although she organized and directed and lectured and discussed, mostly she led by example. For anyone who knew her—kin, colleague, student, friend—she epitomized

158

integrity and courage. Throughout her life she did what needed doing without ever counting the cost. Sally died last summer, too soon by far, no less courageously than she lived. Death came not very long after she put the final touches to this text. For Sally, of course, text finished remained a long way from work completed. Results still need broadcasting, courses of action still needed plotting, new research needed doing. Perhaps *Pleasure, Power, and Technology* will serve some of these ends; perhaps other activists will find their paths a little clearer. And perhaps other sociologists will venture further into the regions she helped chart. In the spirit of Mary Ellen Lease, the legendary Kansas populist[3] she met while writing this book, I'm sure Sally would urge them to raise less fog and more hell.

Bartron C. Hacker
Corvallis,
September 1988

NOTES

[1] Sally Hacker chaired NOW's AT&T Task Force during the early 1970s. Task force papers, as well as related personal papers, have been deposited in the Schlesinger Library. We plan to add other material in the near future, including the data from her survey of MIT faculty members. Contact Curator of Manuscripts, Schlesinger Library, Radcliffe College, 10 Garden Street, Cambridge, MA 02138. Telephone (617) 495–8647.

[2] Dorothy Smith is editing a volume of Sally's articles. She also conducted a lengthy interview with Sally on 29–31 July 1987, extensive excerpts from which will serve as introductions to the book's several sections. Contact Dorothy E. Smith, Department of Sociology in Education, Ontario Institute for Studies in Education, 252 Bloor St. W., Toronto, Ontario, Canada M5S 1V6. Telephone (416) 923–6641.

[3] As a recent biographer comments, an "aura of legend and folk myth clings to accounts of Mrs. Lease's role in the Populist crusade," including even her name. Not only was her real name Mary Elizabeth Lease, but her famous line may have been coined by a hostile reporter (Paulson 1971:381). The legend sounds better.

REFERENCES

Acker, Joan (1980) "Women and Stratification: A Review of Recent Literature." *Contemporary Sociology* 9:25–29.

Acker, Joan (1982) "Editorial Introduction." [Special issue on Women, Work, and Democracy in Working Life, J. Acker, ed.] *Economic and Industrial Democracy* 3 (Nov.):i–viii.

Acker, Joan (1987) "Hierarchies and Jobs: Notes for a Theory of Gendered Organizations." Paper presented at the meetings of the American Sociological Association, Chicago.

Acker, Joan and Donald R. Van Houten (1974) "Differential Recruitment and Control: The Sex Structuring of Organizations." *Administrative Science Quarterly* 19:152–163.

Ambrose, Stephen E. (1966) *Duty, Honor, Country: A History of West Point*. Baltimore: Johns Hopkins University Press.

Ames Daily Tribune (1974) "The reason? It's hexed!" Letter to the Editor. Ames, IA:July 18.

Arregui, Begoña (1986) "Fertility Variations in the Basque Country, 1960–1980." Master's thesis, Demography. London School of Economics.

Asamblea de Trabajadores de Cooperativas y Koperatibisten Taldeak (1986) *Estatuto Berriak Direla Eta*. Leaflet, March.

Azurmendi, Joxe (1984) *El hombre cooperativo: pensamiento de Arizmendiarrieta*. Mondragon: Caja Laboral Popular.

Bambara, Toni Cade (1981) *The Salt Eaters*. New York: Random House.

Barrett, Michele and Mary McIntosh (1982) *The Anti-Social Family*. London: NLB.

Baumann, Eleen (1987) "From Tupperware to 'Loverware': Sociability, Commerce and Eroticism at the Home Sales Parties." Paper presented at the annual meetings of the Popular Culture Association, Montreal.

Bemis, Edward W. (1888) "Coöperation in New England" and "Coöperation in the Middle States." *Johns Hopkins University Studies in Historical and Political Science*, 6th series "History of Cooperation in the United States" Nos. 1, 2, 3.

Benenson, Harold (1984) "Victorian Sexual Ideology and Marx's Theory of the Working Class." *International Labor and Working Class History* 25 (Spring):1–23.

Berg, Anne-Marie (1987) Review of Alice H. Cook, Val R. Lorwin, and Arlene Kaplan Daniels, *Women and the Trade Unions in Eleven Industrialized Countries*. *Economic and Industrial Democracy* 8:259–261.

Bernard, Jessie (1981) *The Female World*. New York: Free Press.

Berman, Katrina V. (1967) *Worker-Owned Plywood Companies: An Economic Analysis*. Bureau of Economic and Business Research Bulletin no. 42, Washington State University, Pullman.

Bernstein, Paul (1976) *Workplace Democratization: Its Internal Dynamics*. Kent, OH: Kent State University Press.

Bernstein, Paul (1982) "Necessary Elements for Effective Worker Participation in Decision-Making." Pp. 51–81 in *Workplace Democracy and Social Change*, edited by Frank Lindenfeld and Joyce Rothschild-Whitt. Boston: Porter Sargent.

Bilbao, Jon (1985) Lectures on Basque history. Universidad de Pais Vasco, Facultad Derecho, San Sebastian.

Black, Donald J. (1976) *The Behavior of Law*. New York: Academic Press.

Bledstein, Burton J. (1976) *The Culture of Professionalism: The Middle Class and the Development of Higher Education in America*. New York: Norton.

Blumberg, Ray Lesser (1976). "Kibbutz Women: From the Fields of Revolution to the Laundries of Discontent." Pp. 319–344 in *Women in the World: A Comparative Study*, edited by Lynne B. Iglitzin and Ruth Ross. Santa Barbara, CA: ABC-Clio.

Bookchin, Murray (1971) *Post-Scarcity Anarchism*. San Francisco: Ramparts.

Bose, Christine (1987) "Devaluing Women's Work: The Under-count of Women's Employment in 1900 and 1980." Pp. 95–115 in *Hidden Aspects of Women's Work*, edited by Christine Bose, Roslyn Feldberg, and Natalie Sokoloff. New York: Praeger.

Boston Women's Health Book Collective (1973) *Our Bodies, Ourselves: A Book by and for Women*. New York: Simon & Schuster.

Boston Women's Health Book Collective (1976) *Nuestros cuerpos, nuestras vidas: Un libro por y para las mujeres*. Somerville, MA: The Collective.

Boulding, Elise (1976) *The Underside of History: A View of Women Through Time*. Boulder, CO: Westview Press.

Bradley, Keith and Alan Gelb (1983) *Cooperation at Work: The Mondragon Experience*. London: Heinemann.

Braverman, Harry (1974) *Labor and Monopoly Capital: The Degradation of Work in the Twentieth Century*. New York: Monthly Review Press.

Briggs, Vernon M., Jr. and the staff of EEOC (1970) *"They Have the Power—We Have the People": The Status of Equal Employment Opportunity in Houston, Texas, 1970.* Washington, DC: Government Printing Office.

Bureau of Labor Statistics (1973) *Outlook for Technology and Manpower in Printing and Publishing.* Bulletin 1774, U.S. Department of Labor. Washington, DC: U.S. Government Printing Office.

Bush, Corlan (Corky) (1981) "Women and Appropriate Technology." Keynote address presented at the 2nd Women's Studies Symposium, Oregon State University, Corvallis.

Calvert, Monte A. (1967) *The Mechanical Engineer in America, 1830–1910: Professional Cultures in Conflict.* Baltimore: Johns Hopkins University Press.

Carden, Maren Lockwood (1974) *The New Feminist Movement.* New York: Russell Sage Foundation.

Cardwell, Donald S. L. (1957) *The Organisation of Science in England: A Retrospect.* London: Heinemann.

Chafetz, Janet Saltzman (1984) *Sex and Advantage: A Comparative Macro-Structural Theory of Sex Stratification.* Totowa NJ: Rowman & Allanheld.

Chase, Elaine R. (1987) *Eye of the Beholder.* New York: Bantam.

Childs, John (1982) *Armies and Warfare in Europe, 1648–1789.* New York: Holmes and Meier.

Cobb, Jonathan and Richard Sennett (1973) *The Hidden Injuries of Class.* New York: Random House.

Cockburn, Cynthia (1983) *Brothers: Male Dominance and Technological Change.* London: Pluto.

Cockburn, Cynthia (1985) *Machinery of Dominance: Women, Men and Technical Know-How.* London: Pluto.

Cockerham, William C. (1973) "Selective Socialization: Airborne Training as Status Passage." *Journal of Political and Military Sociology* 1 (Fall):215–229.

Cockerham, William C. (1977) "Green Berets: Social Cohesion in a Closed Society." In *Our Sociological Eye: Personal Essays on Society and Culture,* edited by Arthur B. Shostak. New York: Alfred.

Cockerham, William C. (1978) "Attitudes Toward Combat Among U.S. Army Paratroopers." *Journal of Political and Military Sociology* 6 (Spring):1–15.

Cohn, Carol (1987) "Sex and Death in the Rational World of Defense Intellectuals." *Signs* 12:687–718.

Collins, Harry M. and Trevor J. Pinch (1982) *Frames of Meaning:*

The Social Construction of Extraordinary Science. Boston: Routledge & Kegan Paul.

Collins, Patricia Hill (1986) "Learning from the Outsider Within: The Sociological Significance of Black Feminist Thought." Special Theory Issue. *Social Problems* 33:S14–S32.

Collins, Roger (1986) *The Basques.* Oxford: Basil Blackwell.

Cooley, Mike (1980) *Architect or Bee? The Human/Technology Relationship.* Boston: South End.

Cooley, Mike (1986) "Socially Useful Design: A Form of Anticipatory Democracy." *Economic and Industrial Democracy* 7:553–559.

Coser, Lewis A. (1978) "American Trends." Pp. 287–320 in *A History of Sociological Analysis*, edited by Tom Bottomore and Robert Nisbet. New York: Basic Books.

Croll, Elizabeth (1982) "The Sexual Division of Labor in Rural China." Pp. 223–247 in *Women and Development: The Sexual Division of Labor in Rural Societies*, edited by Lourdes Beneria. New York: Praeger.

Cummings, Bernice and Victoria Schuck, eds. (1979) *Women Organizing: An Anthology.* Metuchen, NJ: Scarecrow.

Dahms, Mona, Lotte Kjaergaard, Inger Lytje, and Gitte Marling, eds. (1986) *Kvinder Øg Teknologi: Konference Rapport.* Aalborg, Denmark: University of Aalborg.

Dahms, Mona, Lone Dirckinck-Holmfeld, Kirsten Grønbaek Hansen, Anette Kolmos, and Janni Nielsen, eds. (1986) *Women Challenge Technology* (3 vols.). Proceedings of the European Conference on Women, Natural Sciences and Technology, University of Aalborg. Aalborg, Denmark.

Daly, Mary (1973) *Beyond God the Father: Toward a Philosophy of Women's Liberation.* Boston: Beacon.

Daniels, Arlene Kaplan (1985) "Good Times and Good Works: The Place of Sociability in the Work of Women Volunteers." *Social Problems* 32:363–374.

Davies, Margaret Llewelyn (1975) *Life as We Have Known It, by Co-operative Working Women.* New York: Norton. (Original work published 1931).

Davis, Chandler (1980) "Where Did Twentieth-Century Mathematics Go Wrong?" Paper presented at the joint meetings of the Society for the History of Technology, History of Science Society, Philosophy of Science Association, and Society for the Social Study of Science, Toronto.

de Lauretis, Teresa (1984) *Alice Doesn't: Feminism, Semiotics, Cinema.* Bloomington: Indiana University Press.

de Lauretis, Teresa (1987) *Technologies of Gender: Essays on Theory, Film, and Fiction.* Bloomington: Indiana University Press.

del Valle, Teresa (1983) "La mujer vasca a través del análisis del espacio: Utilización y significado," *Lurralde* 6:251–269.

del Valle, Teresa, Joxemartin Apalategi, Begoña Aretxaga, Begoña Arregui, Isabel Babace, Mari C. Díez, Carmen Larrañaga, Amparo Oiarzabal, Carmen Pérez, and Itziar Zuriarrain (1985) *Mujer vasca: Imagen y realidad.* Barcelona: Anthropos.

Derber, Charles and William Schwartz (1983) "Toward a Theory of Worker Participation." *Sociological Inquiry* 53:61–78.

Deutsch, Steven, Donald Van Houten, Paul Goldman, Joan Acker, and Daniel Goldrich (1986) "Review of Bernhard Wilpert and Arndt Sorge, eds., *International Yearbook of Organizational Democracy,* Vol. 2," *Economic and Industrial Democracy* 7:109–117.

D'Onofrio-Flores, Pamela M. and Sheila M. Pfafflin, eds. (1982) *Scientific-Technological Change and the Role of Women in Development.* Boulder, CO: Westview.

Dupuy, Richard E. (1958) *Sylvanus Thayer.* West Point, NY: Association of Graduates.

Easlea, Brian (1983) *Fathering the Unthinkable: Masculinity, Scientists and the Nuclear Arms Race.* London: Pluto.

Edwards, Paul (1985) "Technologies of the Mind: Computers, Power, Psychology, and World War II." Working Paper No. 2. Santa Cruz: Silicon Valley Research Group, University of California.

Edwards, Paul (1986a) "Artificial Intelligence and High Technology War: The Perspective of the Formal Machine." Working Paper No. 6. Santa Cruz: Silicon Valley Research Group, University of California.

Edwards, Paul (1986b) "Border Wars: The Science and Politics of Artificial Intelligence." *Radical America.* 19(6):39–50.

Edwards, Paul (forthcoming) "The Army and the Microworld: Computers and the Militarized Politics of Gender Identity." *Signs.*

Ehrenreich, Barbara and Annette Fuentes (1981) "Life on the Global Assembly Line." *Ms.* (January):53–59, 71.

Ehrenreich, Barbara, Elizabeth Hess, and Gloria Jacobs (1986) *Re-making Love: The Feminization of Sex.* Garden City, NY: Anchor.

Eisentein, Zillah R. (1983) *The Radical Future of Liberal Feminism.* New York: Longman.

Ellerman, David (1982) "On the Legal Structure of Workers' Cooperatives." Pp. 229–314 in *Workplace Democracy and Social*

Change, edited by Frank Lindenfeld and Joyce Rothschild-Whitt. Boston: Porter Sargent.

Enloe, Cynthia (1983) *Does Khaki Become You? The Militarization of Women's Lives*. Boston: South End.

Enroe, Philip C. (1981) "Cambridge University and the Adoption of Analytics in Early 19th Century Mathematics." Pp. 135–148 in *Social History of Nineteenth Century Mathematics*, edited by Herbert Mehrtens, Henk Bos, and Ivo Schneider. Boston: Birkhäuser.

Feldberg, Roslyn (1981) "Women, Self-Management, and Socialism." *Socialist Review* No. 56:[Vol. II no. 2]: 141–152.

Feldberg, Roslyn, and Evelyn Nakano Glenn (1979) "Male and Female: Job Versus Gender Models in the Sociology of Work." *Social Problems* 26:524–538.

Ferguson, Eugene (1977) "The Mind's Eye: Nonverbal Thought in Technology." *Science* 197:827–836.

Ferguson, Kathy E. (1984) *The Feminist Case Against Bureaucracy*. Philadelphia: Temple University Press.

Fetherling, Dale (1974) *Mother Jones, the Miners' Angel: A Portrait*. Carbondale and Edwardsville: Southern Illinois University Press.

Firestone, Shulamith (1970) *The Dialectic of Sex: The Case for Feminist Revolution*. New York: Bantam.

Fleming, Thomas J. (1969) *West Point: The Men and Times of United States Military Academy*. New York: William Morrow.

Florman, Samuel C. (1976) *The Existential Pleasures of Engineering*. New York: St. Martin's.

Florman, Samuel C. (1987) *The Civilized Engineer*. New York: St. Martin's.

Fonow, Mary Margaret and Judith A. Cook, eds. (forthcoming) *Feminist Research Techniques and Strategies for the Study of Gender*. Bloomington: University of Indiana Press.

Foucault, Michel (1978–1986) *The History of Sexuality*. Translated by Robert Hurley. 3 vols. New York: Pantheon.

Foucault, Michel (1979) *Discipline and Punish: The Birth of the Prison*. Translated by Alan Sheridan. New York: Vintage.

Freeman, Jo (1975) *The Politics of Women's Liberation: A Case Study of an Emerging Social Movement and Its Relation to the Policy Process*. New York: David McKay.

Fricke, Werner (1986) "New Technologies and German Co-Determination." *Economics and Industrial Democracy* 7:541–552.

Friedman, Samuel R. (1984) "The Rebirth of Working Class Socialism." Paper presented at the meeting of the American Sociological Association, San Antonio.

Fuentes, Annette and Barbara Ehrenreich (1983) *Women in the*

Global Factory. Institute for New Communications Pamphlet No. 2. Boston: South End.

Fusfield, Daniel R. (1983) "Labor-Managed and Participatory Firms: A Review Article." *Journal of Economic Issues* 17:769–789.

Garcia-Diego, José A. (1984) "Les roues hydrauliques en pierre au Pays Basque." *Boletin de la Real Sociedad Bascongada de los Amigos del Pais* 40:159–201.

Garcia-Diego, José A. (1985a) "El Masonismo de Fausto de Elhuyar y de algunos otros socios de la Bascongada." *Boletin de la Real Sociedad Bascongada de los Amigos del Pais* 41:441–457.

Garcia-Diego, José A. (1985b) *En busca de Betancourt y Lanz*. Madrid: Editorial Castalia.

Garson, Barbara (1975) *All The Livelong Day: The Meaning and Demeaning of Routine Work*. Garden City, NY: Doubleday.

Giese, Paula (1982) "How the Old Coops Went Wrong." Pp. 315–335 in *Workplace Democracy and Social Change*, edited by Frank Lindenfeld and Joyce Rothschild-Whitt. Boston: Porter Sargent.

Gillman, Daniel F. (1983) "Military Is Also in Education Business." *Los Angeles Times* (May 5): Part I-Q, 7.

Glazer, Nona (1984) "Servants to Capital: Unpaid Domestic Labor and Paid Work." *Review of Radical Political Economy* 16:61–87.

Glenn, Evelyn Nakano, and Charles M. Tolbert (1987) "Race and Gender in High Technology Employment: Recent Trends in Computer Occupations." Paper presented at the meeting of the Society for the Study of Social Problems, Chicago.

Glick, Thomas (1970) Joint review of Manuel Lora Tamayo, *Un clima para la ciencia;* Daniel Artigues, *El Opus Dei en España;* OECD, *National Reports of the Pilot Teams, Science and Development, Spain;* Ministerio de Educación y Ciencia, *La educación en España: Bases para una política educativa. Technology and Culture* 11:113–118.

Glick, Thomas (1975) Joint review of Luís Cervera Vera, *El "ingenio" creado por Juan de Herrera para cortar hierro;* Pedro Bernardo Villareal de Berriz, *Máquinas hidraúlicas de molinos y herrerías y govierno de los árboles y montes de Vizcaya;* and Rafael Viravens Pastor, *El Pantano de Tibi. Technology and Culture* 16:293–294.

Gobierno Vasco, Departamento de Educación y Cultura (1983) *Situación de la mujer en Euskadi*. Vitoria-Gasteiz: Uztalia.

Goodwyn, Lawrence (1978) *The Populist Movement: A Short History of the Agrarian Revolt in America*. New York: Oxford University Press.

Gouldner, Alvin W. (1970) *The Coming Crisis of Western Sociology*. New York: Basic Books.

Gouldner, Alvin W. (1976) *The Dialetic of Ideology and Technology: The Origins, Grammar, and Future of Ideology*. New York: Seabury.

Graubard, Allen (1984) "Ideas of Economic Democracy: Workers' Control and Public Rights." *Dissent* 31 (Fall):415–423.

Green, Susan (1983) "Silicon Valley's Women Workers: A Theoretical Analysis of Sex-Segregation in the Electronics Industry Labor Market." Pp. 273–331 in *Women, Men, and the International Division of Labor*, edited by June Nash and María Patricia Fernańdez Kelly. Albany: SUNY Press.

Greenberg, Edward S. (1986) *Workplace Democracy: The Political Effects of Participation*. Ithaca, NY: Cornell University Press.

Greenwood, Davyyd J. (1976) *Unrewarding Wealth*. London: Cambridge University Press.

Griffin, Susan (1978) *Woman and Nature: The Roaring Inside Her*. New York: Harper & Row.

Griffin, Susan (1981) *Pornography and Silence: Culture's Revolt Against Nature*. New York: Harper & Row.

Grossman, Rachael (1980) "Women's Place in the Integrated Circuit." *Radical America* 14(1):29–50.

Gui, Benedetto (1984) "Basque versus Illyrian Labor-Managed Firms: The Problem of Property Rights." *Journal of Comparative Economics* 8:168–181.

Gunn, Christopher Eaton (1984) *Worker's Self Management in the United States*. Ithaca, NY: Cornell University Press.

Hacker, Barton C. (1977) "The Prevalance of War and the Oppression of Women: An Essay on Armies and the Origin of States." Paper presented at the International Conference on Women and Power, University of Maryland, College Park.

Hacker, Barton C. (1981) "Women and Military Institutions in Early Modern Europe: A Reconnaissance." *Signs* 6:643–671.

Hacker, Barton C. (1986) "Nineteenth-Century Military Institutions and Technical Education." Paper presented at the Symposium on Technology and Technical Sciences in History, Dresden, East Germany.

Hacker, Barton C. (1987) "The Invention of Armies: Origins of Military Institutions, Gender Stratification, and the Labor Process." Paper presented at the annual meeting of the Society for the Study of Social Problems, Chicago.

Hacker, Barton C. (1988) "From Military Revolution to Industrial Revolution: Armies, Women, and Political Economy in Early Modern Europe." Pp. 11–29 in *Women and the Military System*, edited by Eva Isaksson. New York: Harvester Wheatsheaf.

Hacker, Barton C. and Sally L. Hacker (1987) "Military Institutions and the Labor Process: Noneconomic Sources of Technological Change, Women's Subordination, and the Organization of Work." *Technology and Culture* 28:743–775.

Hacker, Sally L. (1969) "Patterns of Work and Leisure: An Investigation of the Relationship between Childhood and Current Styles of Leisure and Current Work Behavior among Young Women Graduates in the Field of Public Education." Doctoral disseration, Sociology, University of Chicago.

Hacker, Sally L. (1973) "Patients' Effect on Mental Health Professionals." *The Gerontologist* 13:54–57.

Hacker, Sally L. (1975) "Social Responsibility and Research Institutions: Bell Telephone Laboratories." Paper presented at the Technology Studies Seminar, MIT, Cambridge, MA.

Hacker, Sally L. (1976) "Zen and the Masculine Art of Motorcycle Maintenance." *Sojourner: Voices from the MIT Women's Community* 1 (February):6.

Hacker, Sally L. (1977a) "Farming out the Home: Women and Agribusiness." *The Second Wave* 5 (Spring/Summer):38–49. (Reprinted in *Women and Food*, edited by Jane Kaplan. Englewood Cliffs, NJ: Prentice-Hall, 1980.)

Hacker, Sally L. (1977b) "Technological Change and Disparate Impact." Paper presented at the annual meeting of the American Association for Affirmative Action, Washington, DC.

Hacker, Sally L. (1978) "The Impact of Technological Change on Minorities in Industry." Paper presented at the Northwest Regional Racial Minorities Conference, Portland State University, Portland, OR.

Hacker, Sally L. (1979a) "Sex Stratification, Technology and Organizational Change: A Longitudinal Case Study of AT&T." *Social Problems* 26:539–557. (Reprinted in *Women and Work: Problems and Perspectives*, edited by Rachel Kahn-Hutt, Arlene Kaplan Daniels, and Richard Colvard. New York: Oxford University Press, 1982.)

Hacker, Sally L. (1979b) "The Body of Engineers: Gender, Hierarchy and Dualism in Classroom Humor." Paper presented at the annual meeting of the American Sociological Association, Boston, MA.

Hacker, Sally L. (1979c) "People's Methodology and Organizational Control of Critical Research: Exploratory Research on Technological Change and Women's Role in Agribusiness."

Paper presented at the annual meetings of the American Sociological Association, Boston, MA.

Hacker, Sally L. (1979d) "Women and Technology." Paper presented at the Conference on Women and Appropriate Technology, Seattle, WA.

Hacker, Sally L (1979e) "Employment and Technological Change in Agribusiness." Paper presented at the Symposium on Rural Justice, University of Tennessee, Knoxville.

Hacker, Sally L. (1979f) "Action Research for Rural Women." Paper presented at the annual meeting of the Rural Sociological Society, Burlington, VT.

Hacker, Sally L. (1980) "Technological Change and Women's Role in Agribusiness." *Human Services in the Rural Environment* 5:6–14.

Hacker, Sally L. (1981a) "The Culture of Engineering: Woman, Workplace and Machine." *Women's Studies International Quarterly* 4:341–353. (Reprinted in *Women, Technology, and Innovation*, edited by Joan Rothschild. New York: Pergamon, 1982).

Hacker, Sally L. (1981b) "Automated and Automators: Human and Social Costs of Technological Change." In International Federation of Automated Control, *Proceedings of the Conference on System Approach to Development, Rabat, Morocco, 1980*. New York: Pergamon.

Hacker, Sally L. (1982) "Agriculture and Human Values: A Feminist Perspective." Paper presented at the Conference on Agriculture and Human Values, University of Florida, Gainesville.

Hacker, Sally L. (1983a) "Mathematization of Engineering: Limits on Women and the Field." Pp. 38–58 in *Machina ex Dea: Feminist Perspectives on Technology*, edited by Joan Rothschild. New York: Pergamon.

Hacker, Sally L. (1983b) "Agriculture and Technology." Paper presented at the University of California Conference on Appropriate Technology, Santa Barbara.

Hacker, Sally L. (1983c) "My Calculus is Bigger Than Yours: Math Testing as a Barrier to the Professions." Paper presented at the annual meeting of the Pacific Sociological Association, San Jose, CA.

Hacker, Sally L. (1983d) "Engineering the Shape of Work." Pp. 300–316 in *Beyond Whistleblowing: Defining Engineers' Responsibilities*, edited by Vivian Weil. Chicago: Illinois Institute of Technology.

Hacker, Sally L. (1984) "Discipline in the Engineering Curriculum." Paper presented to the Faculty Seminar, Program on Science, Technology, Society, and Values, Stanford University, Stanford, CA.

Hacker, Sally L. (1985) "Doing It the Hard Way: Ethnographic Study of Ideology in Agribusiness and Engineering Classes." *Humanity and Society* 9:123–141.

Hacker, Sally L. (1986a) "Turning Young Boys into Men: Technique and Engineering Education." Paper presented at the annual meeting of the Organization of American Historians, New York.

Hacker, Sally L. (1986b) "Technological Development in a Patriarchal Society." Pp. 40–55 in *Kvinder øg Teknologi: Konference Rapport*, edited by Mona Dahms, Lotte Kjaergaard, Inger Lytje, and Gitte Marling. Scandinavian Conference on Women, Technology, and Science, University of Aalborg, Denmark.

Hacker, Sally L. (1987a) "Women Workers in the Mondragon System of Industrial Cooperatives." *Gender and Society* 1:358–379.

Hacker, Sally L. (1987b) "Feminist Perspectives on Computer Based Systems and Democracy at the Workplace." Pp. 177–190 in *Computers and Democracy: A Scandinavian Challenge*, edited by Gro Bjerkness, Pelle Ehn, and Morten Kyng. Aldershot, Hants.: Avebury.

Hacker, Sally L. (1987c) "Women Workers and Technology in the Cooperative Workplace." Paper presented in the program on Social Interpretation of Technics, Inter-University Centre of Postgraduate Studies, Dubrovnik, Yugoslavia.

Hacker, Sally L. (1987d) "The Eye of the Beholder: Feminist Debates on Technology and Pornography." Paper prepared for the Third International Interdisciplinary Congress on Women, University of Dublin, Ireland.

Hacker, Sally L. (1988) "Gender and Technology at the Mondragon System of Producer Cooperatives." *Economic and Industrial Democracy* 9:225–243.

Hacker, Sally L., Eleen Baumann, Dorice Tentchoff, Jule Wind, and Sutree Irving (1984). "Some Material and Ideological Bases of the Radical Sex Controversy." Paper presented at the annual meetings of the Society for the Study of Social Problems, San Antonio, TX.

Hacker, Sally L. and Lisa Bovit (1982) "Agriculture to Agribusiness: Technical Imperatives and Changing Roles." Pp. 47–57 in *The History and Sociology of Technology: Proceedings of the Twenty-Fourth Annual Meeting of the Society for the History of Technology, Milwaukee, Wisconsin, October 14–17, 1981*, edited by Donald Hoke. Milwaukee: Milwaukee Public Museum.

Hacker, Sally L. and Charles M. Gaitz (1969) "The Moral Career of the Elderly Mental Patient." *The Gerontologist* 9:120–127.

Hacker, Sally L. and Charles M. Gaitz (1970) "Interaction and Performance Correlates of Machiavellianism." *Sociological Quarterly* 11:94–102.

Hacker, Sally L., Charles M. Gaitz, and Barton C. Hacker (1972) "A Humanistic View of Measuring Mental Health." *Journal of Humanistic Psychology* 12:94–106.

Hacker, Sally L. and Barton C. Hacker (1983) "Regimenting Labor: Military Institutions and the Organization of Work." Paper presented at the annual meetings of the Society for the Study of Social Problems, Detroit, MI.

Hacker, Sally L. and Barton C. Hacker (1984) "Women and the History of Military Technology: Reflections on Gender Roles, Engineering Education, and Military Institutions." Pp. 377–380 in *George Sarton Centennial, University of Ghent, Belgium, 14–17 November 1984*, edited by Werner Callebaut, Susan E. Cozzens, Bernard-Pierre Lecuyer, Arie Rip, and Jean Paul Van Bendegem. Ghent: Communication & Cognition.

Hacker, Sally L. and Charles E. Starnes (1983) "Computers in the Workplace: Stratification and Labor Process among Engineers and Technicians." Paper presented at the Conference on Microelectronics in Transition, University of California, Santa Cruz.

Hanawalt, Barbara A., ed. (1986) *Women and Work in Preindustrial Europe*. Bloomington: Indiana University Press.

Haraway, Donna J. (1981–1982) "The High Cost of Information in Post-World War II Evolutionary Biology: Ergonomics, Semiotics, and the Sociobiology of Communication Systems." *Philosophical Forum* 13:244–278.

Haraway, Donna J. (1985) "A Manifesto for Cyborgs: Science, Technology, and Socialist Feminism in the 1980s." *Socialist Review* No. 80, 65–125.

Harding, Sandra (1986) *The Science Question in Feminism*. Ithaca, NY: Cornell University Press.

Harrison, Joseph (1983) "Heavy Industry, the State, and Economic Development in the Basque Region, 1876–1936." *Economic History Review* Ser. 2, 36:535–551.

Hartmann, Heidi I. (1977) "Capitalism, Patriarchy, and Job Segregation." Pp. 71–84 in *Women in a Man-Made World: A Socioeconomic Handbook*, edited by Nona Glazer-Malbin and Helen Youngelson Waeher. 2nd ed. Chicago: Rand McNally.

Hartmann, Heidi I., Robert E. Kraut, and Louis A. Tilly, eds. (1986) *Computer Chips and Paper Clips: Technology and Women's*

Employment. 2 vols. Washington, DC: National Academy Press.

Hartzell, Hal, Jr. (1987) *Birth of a Cooperative: Hoedads, Inc., A Worker Owned Forest Labor Co-op.* Eugene, OR: Hulogos'i Communications.

Heydebrand, Wolf (1985) "Technocratic Administration: Beyond Weber's Bureaucracy." Unpublished manuscript, Department of Sociology, New York University.

Heyzer, Noeleen (1986) *Working Women in South-East Asia: Development, Subordination and Emancipation.* Philadelphia: Open University Press.

Hole, Judith and Ellen Levine (1971) *Rebirth of Feminism.* New York: Quandrangle Books.

Hooks, Bell (1981) *Ain't I A Woman? Black Women and Feminism.* Boston: South End.

Hoos, Ida R. (1972) *Systems Analysis in Public Policy: A Critique.* Berkeley: University of California Press.

Hounshell, David A. (1984) *From the American System to Mass Production, 1800–1932: The Development of Manufacturing Technology in the United States.* Baltimore: Johns Hopkins University Press.

Howell, Martha C. (1986) "Women, the Family Economy, and the Structures of Market Production in Cities of Northern Europe during the Late Middle Ages." Pp. 198–222 in *Women and Work in Preindustrial Europe*, edited by Barbara A. Hanawalt. Bloomington: Indiana University Press.

Huber, Joan and Glenna Spitze (1983) *Sex Stratification: Children, Housework, and Jobs.* New York: Academic Press.

Isely, Barbara J. (1988) *Modernization and Sex Differences in Mortality in India: A New Perspective.* Working Papers on Women in International Development. East Lansing: Office of Women in International Development, Michigan State University.

ISIS: Women's International Information and Communication Service (1984) *Women in Development: A Resource Guide for Organization and Action.* Philadelphia: New Society.

Jackall, Robert and Joyce Crain (1984) "The Shape of the Small Worker Cooperative Movement." Pp. 88–108 in *Worker Cooperatives in America*, edited by Robert Jackall and Henry M. Levin. Berkeley: University of California Press.

Jackall, Robert and Henry M. Levin, eds. (1984) *Worker Cooperatives in America.* Berkeley: University of California Press.

Jaggar, Alison M. (1983) *Feminist Politics and Human Nature.* Totowa, NJ: Rowman & Allanheld.

Jansson, June and Ann-Britt Hellmark, eds. (1986) *Labor-Owned Firms and Workers' Cooperatives*. Brookfield, VT: Gower.

Johnson, Ana Gutierrez (1978) "Women and Self-Management." Unpublished manuscript, School of Industrial Relations, Cornell University, Ithaca, NY.

Johnson, Ana Gutierrez and William Foote Whyte (1982) "The Mondragon System of Worker Production Cooperatives." Pp. 177–197 in *Workplace Democracy and Social Change*, edited by Frank Lindenfeld and Joyce Rothschild-Whitt. Boston: Porter Sargent.

Jones, Derek C. and Donald J. Schneider (1984) "Self-Help Production: Government-Administered Cooperatives during the Depression." Pp. 57–84 in *Worker Cooperatives in America*, edited by Robert Jackall and Henry M. Levin. Berkeley: University of California Press.

Kahn-Hutt, Rachel, Arlene Kaplan Daniels, and Richard Colvard, eds. (1982) *Women and Work: Problems and Perspectives*. New York: Oxford University Press.

Kandiyoti, Deniz (1984) "Women and Society." Address on women and development presented at Oregon State University, Corvallis.

Kandiyoti, Deniz (1987) "The Problem of Subjectivity in Western Feminist Theory." Paper presented at the meetings of the American Sociological Association, Chicago.

Kanter, Rosabeth Moss (1975) "Women and the Structure of Organizations: Explorations in Theory and Behavior." In *Another Voice: Feminist Perspectives on Social Life and Social Science*, edited by Marcia Millman and Rosabeth Moss Kanter. Garden City, NY: Anchor.

Kanter, Rosabeth Moss (1979) *Men and Women of the Corporation*. New York: Basic Books.

Kanter, Rosabeth Moss, Barry A. Stein, and Derick W. Brinkerhoff (1982) "Building Participatory Democracy within a Conventional Corporation." Pp. 371–382 in *Workplace Democracy and Social Change*, edited by Frank Lindenfeld and Joyce Rothschild-Whitt. Boston: Porter Sargent.

Kaplan, E. Ann (1983) "Is the Gaze Male?" Pp. 309–327 in *Powers of Desire: The Politics of Sexuality*, edited by Ann Snitow, Christine Stansell, and Sharon Thompson. New York: Monthly Review Press.

Keller, Evelyn Fox (1985) *Reflections on Gender and Science*. New Haven, CT: Yale University Press.

Kelly, María Patricia Fernández (1983) "Mexican Border Indus-

trialization, Female Labor Force Participation, and Migration."
Pp. 205–223 in *Women, Men and the International Division of Labor*, edited by June Nash and Maria Patricia Fernández Kelly. Albany: SUNY Press.

Kidder, Tracy (1981) *The Soul of a New Machine*. New York: Avon.

Kimmel, Michael S. (1987) "Men's Response to Feminism at the Turn of the Century." *Gender and Society* 1:261–283.

Kolodny, Annette (1975) *The Lay of the Land: Metaphor as Experience and History in American Life and Letters*. Chapel Hill: University of North Carolina Press.

Kornegger, Peggy (1975) "Anarchism: The Feminist Connection." *The Second Wave* 4(Spring):26–37.

Kraft, Philip and Steven Dubnoff (1983) "Software Workers Survey." *Computer World* (November):3, 5, 6, 8–13.

Kravitz, Linda (1974) *Who's Minding The Co-op? A Report on Farmer Control of Farmer Cooperatives*. Washington, DC: Agribusiness Accountability Project.

Lakey, George (1987) *Powerful Peacemaking: A Strategy for a Living Revolution*. Rev. ed. Philadelphia: New Society.

Lamphere, Louise (1984) "On the Shop Floor: Multi-Ethnic Unity Against the Conglomerate." Pp. 247–263 in *My Troubles Are Going to Have Trouble With Me: Everyday Trials and Triumphs of Women Workers*, edited by Karen Brodkin Sacks and Dorothy Remy. New Brunswick, NJ: Rutgers University Press.

Larrañaga, Ramiro (1981) *Sintesis historica de la armeria vasca*. San Sebastian: Caja de Ahorros Provincial de Guipuzcoa.

Layton, Edwin (1969) "Science, Business and the American Engineer." Pp. 51–72 in *The Engineers and the Social System*, edited by Robert Perrucci and Joel E. Gerstl. New York: Wiley.

Layton, Edwin (1971) "Mirror-Image Twins: The Communities of Science and Technology in 19th-Century America." *Technology and Culture* 12:562–580.

Lehrer, Susan (1987) *Origins of Protective Labor Legislation for Women, 1905–1925*. Albany: SUNY Press.

Lehrer, Tom (1981) *Too Many Songs by Tom Lehrer with Not Enough Drawings by Ronald Searle*. New York: Pantheon.

Lerner, Gerda (1986) *The Creation of Patriarchy*. New York: Oxford University Press.

Levy, Steven (1985) *Hackers: Heroes of the Computer Revolution*. New York: Dell.

Lilienfeld, Robert (1978) *The Rise of Systems Theory: An Ideological Analysis*. New York: Wiley.

Lindenfeld, Frank (1986) "Routes to Social Change." *Social Anarchism* 6(1):5–14.

Lindenfeld, Frank, and Joyce Rothschild-Whitt, eds. (1982) *Workplace Democracy and Social Change.* Boston: Porter Sargent.

Lytje, Inger, ed. (1985) *Proceedings, Conference on Gender and Technology.* Denmark: Aalborg University.

Maccoby, Eleanor E.(1963) "Women's Intellect." Pp. 24–39 in *The Potential of Woman,* edited by Seymour M. Farber and Roger H. L. Wilson. New York: McGraw-Hill.

McGuire, John (1984) Article in *Student Service News* (Oregon State University) (Winter).

Mann, Charles R. (1918) *A Study of Engineering Education.* Carnegie Foundation for the Advancement of Teaching. Bulletin No. 11. New York.

Melman, Seymour (1974) *The Permanent War Economy: American Capitalism in Decline.* New York: Simon & Schuster.

Melman, Seymour (1987) *Conversion from Military to Civilian Economy: An Economic Alternative to the Arms Race.* Washington, DC: National SANE Education Fund.

Mendizabel, Antxon (1985) Private communication. Mondragon.

Merchant, Carolyn (1980) *The Death of Nature: Women, Ecology, and the Scientific Revolution.* San Franscisco: Harper & Row.

Mernissi, Fatima (1987) *Beyond the Veil: Male-Female Dynamics in a Modern Muslim Society.* Bloomington: Indiana University Press.

Middendorff, Nadine Archer (1987) "CLA Close-Up: Sally Hacker." *CLA Alum: The Magazine for Alumni of the OSU College of Liberal Arts* 3(Winter):1–3.

Morgan, Robin (1970) *Sisterhood Is Powerful: An Anthology of Writings from the Women's Liberation Movement.* New York: Random House.

Morison, Toni (1970) *The Bluest Eyes.* New York: Pocket Books.

Morrison, James Lunsford, Jr. (1970) "The U.S. Military Academy, 1833–1860: Years of Progress and Turmoil." Doctoral dissertation, History, Columbia University.

Mumford, Lewis (1967–1970) *The Myth of the Machine* (Vol. I, *Technics and Human Development:* Vol. II, *The Pentagon of Power*). New York: Harcourt Brace Jovanovich.

Mumford, Lewis (1972) "Technics and the Nature of Man." Pp. 77–85 in *Philosophy and Technology: Readings in the Philosophical Problems of Technology,* edited by Carl Mitcham and Robert Mackey. New York: Free Press.

Nash, June and María Patricia Fernández Kelly, eds. (1983) *Women, Men, and the International Division of Labor.* Albany: SUNY Press.

175

Nazzari, Muriel (1983) "The 'Woman Question' in Cuba: An Analysis of Material Constraints on Its Solution." *Signs* 9:246–263.

Nenninger, Timothy K. (1978) *The Leavenworth Schools and the Old Army: Education, Professionalism, and the Officer Corps of the United States Army, 1881–1918.* Westport, CT: Greenwood.

Neumann, A. Lin (1978–1979) "'Hospitality Girls' in the Philippines." Special joint issue of *Southeast Asia Chronicle* No. 66; and *Pacific Research* 9(5–6):18–23.

Nielsen, Joyce McCarl (1978) *Sex in Society: Perspectives on Stratification.* Belmont, CA: Wadsworth.

Noble, David F. (1977) *America by Design: Science, Technology and the Rise of Corporate Capitalism.* New York: Knopf.

Noble, David F. (1984) *Forces of Production: A Social History of Industrial Automation.* New York: Knopf.

Noble, David F. (Forthcoming) *A World without Women: The Masculinization of Western Science and Technology.* New York: Knopf.

Noun, Louise (1969) *Strong-Minded Women: The Emergence of the Women-Suffrage Movement in Iowa.* Ames: Iowa State University Press.

Noun, Louise (1974) Open letter to the United Way board of directors and citizens of Des Moines, June 21.

NOW (1974) "Voluntarism Is Seen as No Cure for Social Ills," statement by Task Force on Voluntarism, Des Moines Chapter, National Organization for Women, in *Des Moines Sunday Register*, Aug. 25.

NSF (1982) *Changing Employment Patterns of Scientists, Engineers, and Technicians in Manufacturing Industries: 1977–80.* Report No. NSF 82–331. Washington, DC: National Science Foundation.

NSF (1984a) *Projected Response of the Science, Engineering, and Technical Labor Market to Defense and Nondefense Needs: 1982–87.* Report No. NSF 84–304. Washington, DC: National Science Foundation.

NSF (1984b) *Scientific and Technical Work Force in Trade and Regulated Industries Shows Major Shift in Occupational Composition: 1979–82.* Washington, DC: National Science Foundation.

Oakeshott, Robert (1978) *The Case for Workers' Co-ops.* London: Routledge & Kegan Paul.

Oakeshott, Robert (1982) *Lagun-Aro: The Non-Profit Making Social Welfare Mutuality of the Mondragon Co-operatives.* Report for Nuffield Foundation. London: Job Ownership Ltd.

O'Connell, Charles F., Jr. (1985) "The Corps of Engineers and the Rise of Modern Management, 1827–1856." In *Military Enterprise and Technological Change: Perspectives on the American Experience,* edited by Merritt Roe Smith. Cambridge: MIT Press.

Ortner, Sherry (1972) "Is Female to Male as Nature Is to Culture?" *Feminist Studies* 1(2):5–31.

Paige, Karen Ericksen and Jeffery M. Paige (1981) *The Politics of Reproductive Ritual.* Berkeley: University of California Press.

Papanek, Hanna (1987) "The World Is Not Like Us: Limits of Feminist Imagination." Paper presented at the meetings of the American Sociological Association, Chicago.

Pateman, Carole (1970) *Participation and Democratic Theory.* New York: Cambridge University Press.

Pateman, Carole (1983) "Some Reflections on *Participation and Democratic Theory.*" Pp. 107–120 in *International Yearbook of Organizational Democracy: For the Study of Participation, Co-operation, and Power,* Vol. I: *Organizational Democracy and Political Processes,* edited by Colin Crouch and Frank A. Heller. New York: Wiley.

Paulson, Ross E. (1971) "LEASE, Mary Elizabeth Clyens." Vol. 2, pp. 380–382 in *Notable American Women, 1607–1950: A Biographical Dictionary,* edited by Edward T. James, Janet Wilson James, and Paul S. Boyer. 3 vols. Cambridge: Belknap Press of Harvard University Press.

Peel, Frank (1968) *The Rising of the Luddites, Chartists and Plug-Drawers.* 4th ed. with Introduction by E. P. Thompson. Reprint of 3rd ed., 1895. London: Frank Cass.

Peiss, Kathy (1986) *Cheap Amusements: Working Women and Leisure in Turn-of-the-Century New York.* Philadelphia: Temple University Press.

Perez de Calleja, Antonio (1982) "The Mondragon Experiment." Working Research Paper Series, 6(3). Ulster Polytechnic, Faculty of Business and Management, School of Applied Economics, Northern Ireland.

Petroski, Henry (1985) *To Engineer Is Human: The Role of Failure in Successful Design.* New York: St. Martin's.

Phillips, Eileen, ed. (1983) *The Left and the Erotic.* London: Lawrence & Wishart.

Phongpaichit, Pasuk (1982) *From Peasant Girls to Bangkok Masseuses.* Women, Work and Development Series 2. Geneva: International Labour Office.

Piercy, Marge (1976) *Woman on the Edge of Time.* New York: Knopf.

Piercy, Marge (1985) *Small Changes.* New York: Fawcett. Reprint of work originally published in 1973.

Pincus, Fred L. (1980) "The False Promise of Community

Colleges: Class Conflict and Vocational Education." *Harvard Educational Review* 50:332–361.

Radzialowski, Thaddeus C. (1978) "'Let Us Join Hands': The Polish Women's Alliance." *Review Journal of Philosophy and Social Science* 2:183–203. (Excerpted, pp. 174–180 in *Immigrant Women*, edited by Maxine Schwartz Seller. Philadelphia: Temple University Press, 1981.)

Rose, Hilary (1983) "Hand, Brain, and Heart: A Feminist Epistemology for the Natural Sciences." *Signs* 9:73–90.

Rosen, Corey M., Katherine H. Klein, and Karen M. Young (1986) *Employee Ownership in America: The Equity Solution.* Lexington, MA: Lexington Books.

Rosenbrock, N. H. (1977) "The Future of Control." *Automatica* 13:389–392.

Rothschild, Joan, ed. (1983) *Machina ex Dea: Feminist Perspectives on Technology.* New York: Pergamon.

Rothschild, Joyce (1987) "Do Collectivist-Democratic Forms of Organization Presuppose Feminism? Cooperative Work Structures and Women's Values." Paper presented at the annual meeting of the American Sociological Association, Chicago.

Rothschild, Joyce and Allen Whitt (1986) *The Cooperative Workplace: Potentials and Dilemmas of Organizational Democracy and Participation.* New York: Cambridge Univeristy Press.

Rothschild-Whitt, Joyce (1982) "The Collectivist Organization: An Alternative to Bureaucratic Models." Pp. 23–50 in *Workplace Democracy and Social Change*, edited by Frank Lindenfeld and Joyce Rothschild-Whitt. Boston: Porter Sargent.

Rozwenc, Edwin Charles (1975) *Cooperatives Come to America: The History of the Protective Union Store Movement, 1845–1867.* Philadelphia: Porcupine.

Russell, Raymond (1982) "The Rewards of Participation in the Worker-Owned Firm." Pp. 109–124 in *Workplace Democracy and Social Change*, edited by Frank Lindenfeld and Joyce Rothschild-Whitt. Boston: Parker Sargent.

Sacks, Karen Brodkin (1984) "Generations of Working Class Families." Pp. 15–38, in *My Troubles Are Going to Have Trouble with Me: Everyday Trials and Triumphs of Women Workers*, edited by Karen Brodkin Sacks and Dorothy Remy. New Brunswick, NJ: Rutgers University Press.

Sacks, Karen Brodkin and Dorothy Remy, eds. (1984) *My Troubles Are Going to Have Trouble with Me: Everyday Trials and Triumphs of Women Workers.* New Brunswick, NJ: Rutgers University Press.

Samois (1982) *Coming to Power: Writings and Graphics on Lesbian S-M.* Boston: Alyson.

Schlesinger, Melinda Bart and Pauline B. Bart (1982) "Collective Work and Self-Identity: Working in a Feminist Illegal Abortion Collective. Pp. 139–156 in *Workplace Democracy and Social Change*, edited by Frank Lindenfeld and Joyce Rothschild-Whitt. Boston: Porter Sargent.

Shapiro-Perl, Nina (1984) "Resistance Strategies: The Routine Struggle for Bread and Roses." Pp. 193–208 in *My Troubles Are Going to Have Trouble with Me: Everyday Trials and Triumphs of Women Workers*, edited by Karen Brodkin Sacks and Dorothy Remy. New Brunswick, NJ: Rutgers University Press.

Shepherd, William G. (1971) "The Competitive Margin in Communications." Pp. 86–122 in *Technological Change in Regulated Industries*, edited by William M. Capron. Washington, DC: Brookings Institution.

Simmel, Georg (1984) "Flirtation." Pp. 133–152 in *Georg Simmel: On Women, Sexuality, and Love*, translated by Guy Oakes. New Haven, CT: Yale University Press (Originally published in 1923).

Sinclair, Bruce (1974) *Philadelphia's Philosopher Mechanics: A History of the Franklin Institute, 1824–1865.* Baltimore: Johns Hopkins University Press.

Smith, Dennis (1988) *The Chicago School: A Liberal Critique of Capitalism.* New York: St. Martin's.

Smith, Dorothy (1974) "Women's Perspective as a Radical Critique of Sociology." *Sociological Inquiry* 44:7–13.

Smith, Judy (1978) *Something Old, Something New, Something Borrowed, Something Due: Women and Appropriate Technology.* NCAT Brief 1(1). Washington, DC: National Center for Appropriate Technology.

Smith, Merritt Roe, ed. (1985) *Military Enterprise and Technological Change: Perspectives on the American Experience.* Cambridge: MIT Press.

Snitow, Ann, Christine Stansell, and Sharon Thompson, eds. (1983) *Powers of Desire: The Politics of Sexuality.* New York: Monthly Review Press.

Snyder, Benson R. (1971) *The Hidden Curriculum.* New York: Knopf.

Sokoloff, Natalie J. (1980) *Between Money and Love: The Dialectics of Woman's Home and Market Work.* New York: Praeger.

Sørensen, Knut H. (1984) "Deconstruction of Systems Analysis: Towards a Semiotics of Engineering." Paper presented at George

Sarton Centennial, University of Ghent, Belgium, November.

Spinrad, Norman (1972) *The Iron Dream*. New York: Avon.

Stacey, Judith (1983) *Patriarchy and Socialist Revolution in China*. Berkeley: University of California Press.

Stacey, Judith (1987) "Sexism by a Subtler Name? Postindustrial Conditions and Postfeminist Consciousness in the Silicon Valley." *Socialist Review* No. 96:7–28.

Stacey, Judith and Barrie Thorne (1985) "The Missing Feminist Revolution in Sociology." *Social Problems* 32:301–316.

Stanley, Autumn (1983) "Women Hold Up Two-Thirds of the Sky." Notes for a Revised History of Technology. Pp. 3–22 in *Machina ex Dea: Feminist Perspectives on Technology*, edited by Joan Rothschild. New York: Pergamon.

Starhawk (1982) *Dreaming the Dark: Magic, Sex, and Politics*. Boston: Beacon.

Steihm, Judith Hicks, ed. (1983) *Women and Men's Wars*. New York: Pergamon.

Stine, Jeffrey K. (1984) "Professionalism vs. Special Interest: The Debate over Engineering Education in Nineteenth-Century America." *Potomac Review* 27:72–94.

Stone, Merlin (1976) *When God Was a Woman*. New York: Harcourt Brace Jovanovich.

Street, John (1983) "Socialist Arguments for Industrial Democracy." *Economic and Industrial Democracy* 4:519–539.

Talmon, Yonina (1972) *Family and Community in the Kibbutz*. Cambridge, MA: Harvard University Press.

Tellechea Idigoras, José Ignacio, ed. (1985) *Plan de una sociedad economica, o academia de agricultura, ciencias, y artes utiles*. San Sebastian: Juntas Generales de Guipuzcoa. (Original work published 1763)

Temas de historia militar (1982) Vol. 1, *Ponencias del Primer Congreso de Historia Militar, Zaragoza*. Madrid: Servicio de Publicaciones del EME.

Thomas, Henck and Chris Logan (1981) *Mondragon: An Economic Analysis*. London: Allen & Unwin.

Thompson, E. P. (1963) *The Making of the English Working Class*. New York: Vintage.

Tienda, Marta, Shelley A. Smith, and Vilma Ortiz (1987) "Industrial Restructuring, Gender Segregation, and Sex Differences in Earnings." *American Sociological Review* 52(April): 195–210.

Tilly, Charles (1986) *The Contentious French*. Cambridge, MA: Belknap Press of Harvard University Press.

Tilly, Louise (1981) "Paths of Proletarianization: Organization of

Production, Sexual Division of Labor, and Women's Collective Action." *Signs* 7:400–417.

Urdangarin, Carmelo and Francisco Aldabaldetrecu (1982) *Historia tecnica y economica de la maquina-herramienta.* San Sebastian: Caja de Ahorros Provincial de Guipúzcoa.

Useem, Elizabeth and Linda Kimball (1983) "High Technology and Challenges to Education: Policies, Dilemmas and Social Inequities." Paper presented at the Conference on Micro-electronics in Transition, University of California, Santa Cruz.

Valverde, Mariana (1987) *Sex, Power and Pleasure.* Philadelphia: New Society.

Vanek, Jaroslav (1977) *The Labor-Managed Economy: Essays.* Ithaca, NY: Cornell University Press.

Villareal de Barriz, Pedro Bernardo (1973) *Maquinas hidraulicas de molinos y herrerias y govierno de los arboles y montes de Vizcaya.* Prolog by José A. Garcia Diego. San Sebastian: Sociedad Guipuzcoana de Edicions y Publicaciones. Fascimile edition of book first published in 1763.

Wajcman, Judy (1983) *Women in Control: Dilemmas of a Workers Co-operative.* New York: St. Martin's.

Wallace, Phyllis A. and Jack E. Nelson (1976) "Legal Processes and Strategies of Intervention." Pp. 243–252 in *Equal Employment Opportunity and the AT&T Case*, edited by Phyllis A. Wallace. Cambridge: MIT Press.

Ward, Kathryn B. (1984) *Women in the World Economic System: Its Impact on Status and Fertility.* Westport, CT: Praeger.

Warner, Amos G. (1888) "Three Phases of Coöperation in the West." Pp. 367–439 in *John Hopkins University Studies in Historical and Political Science.* 6th series, "History of Cooperation in the United States" Nos. 7, 8.

Weber, Max (1968) *Economy and Society: An Outline of Interpretive Sociology* (2 vols.), translated by Ephraim Fischoff and others, edited by Guenther Roth and Claus Wittich (from the German 4th ed.). New York: Bedminster.

Weeks, John R. (1986) *Population: An Introduction to Concepts and Issues.* 3rd ed. Belmont, CA: Wadsworth.

Weizenbaum, Joseph (1976) *Computer Power and Human Reason: From Judgment to Calculation.* San Francisco: W. H. Freeman.

Whyte, Judith (1986) *Girls into Science and Technology: The Story of a Project.* London: Routledge & Kegan Paul.

Whyte, William Foote (1982) "Social Inventions for Solving Human Problems: American Sociological Association, 1981 Presidential Address." *American Sociological Review* 47:1–13.

Whyte, William Foote (1986) "On the Uses of Social Science

Research." *American Sociological Review* 51:555–563.

Wickenden, William E. (1930–1934) *Report of the Investigation of Engineering Education, 1923–1929, Accompanied by Supplemental Report on Technical Institutes, 1928–1929* (2 vols.). Pittsburgh: Society for the Promotion of Engineering Education.

Willis, Paul (1977) *Learning to Labour: How Working Class Kids Get Working Class Jobs*. Farnborough: Saxon House.

Winner, Langdon (1977) *Autonomous Technology: Technics-Out-of-Control as a Theme in Political Thought*. Cambridge: MIT Press.

Woodward, C. Vann (1971) "Blacks and Poor Whites in the South." Pp. 53–77 in *The Underside of American History: Other Readings* (Vol. II), edited by Thomas R. Fraizer. New York: Harcourt Brace Jovanovich.

Woolf, Virginia (1975) "Introductory letter to Margaret Llewelyn Davies," dated May 1930. Pp. xv-xxxix in *Life As We Have Known It, by Co-operative Working Women*, edited by Margaret Llewelyn Davies. New York: Norton.

Zubillaga, Teresa (1987) "Mujeres antimilitaristas en Euskadi." Paper presented at the International Symposium on Women and the Military System, Siuntio Baths, Finland.

Zwerdling, Daniel (1982) "At IGP, It's Not Business as Usual." Pp. 221–240 in *Workplace Democracy and Social Change*, edited by Frank Lindenfeld and Joyce Rothschild-Whitt. Boston: Porter Sargent.

INDEX

Abuse, of women and children, 50
Academic measures, as predictors of
    engineering performance, 67–8
Activism, in small groups, 145–7
Affirmative action, by AT&T, 19–20
Agrarian alliances, 81
Agribusiness classes, 30
Agricultural societies, 10
Agriculture, technological displacement
    and, 28
Alienation, in engineering courses, 44
American Telephone and Telegraph
    (AT&T/
    affirmative action by, 19–20
    civil rights settlement against, 22
    discrimination against women by, 19
    involvement in defense systems, 58–9
    social organization of, 24
Anarchism, social, 13–14, 86
Arizmendi, Father 92
Armies, early modern, 60
Authoritarian technics, 125–7
Automation
    costs under co-ops, 106
    women and minorities as easing the
        path of, 25
    women's jobs and, 21
Auzo lagun, 91

Basque culture, 108, 110–19
    Catholic church in, 117
    contradictions in, 129–31
    education in, 117
    egalitarianism in, 111–12
    gender differentiation in, 114–16
    individualism in, 112
    marriage in, 116–17
    matriarchal aspects of, 116
    militarization of women in, 118
    radical women's groups in, 113–14
    sexuality in, 115–16
    social life in, 112, 113
    solidarity in, 144

    women's groups in, 115–16
Basque engineering, 124
Basque technology, gender in the history
    of, 122–4
Beauty pageants, 141–3
Black cooperatives, 81
Bureaucracy
    hierarchical structure of, 48
    masculinity and, 57
Bureaucratic organizations, versus
    cooperatives, 88

Caja Laboral Popular, 91, 92–3
Capital, military state and, 59
Capitalism
    co-op survival under, 87–8
    exploitation and, 12
    labor costs and, 24
Catholic church
    in Basque culture, 117
    effect on Basque technology, 122
"Catholicization of science," 122–3
Chicana farmers, 29
Child abuse, 50
Child care
    collective models of, 137
    responsibility for, in co-ops, 136
    women's responsibility for, 109
China, socialist revolution in, 109
Civil engineering, 35, 61
Civilian labor regulations, 61
Cockburn, Cynthia, 6, 45
Collectives, 14
"Command" technologies, 65
Communication, patterns of, 144–5
Competition, among U.S. engineering
    students, 128
Computer science, 35
Consumer cooperatives, 77
Contentiousness, effectiveness of, 140–1
Cooley's Technology Centers, 149
Cooperation
    conflict and, 15–16